ENDORSEMENTS

"Pastor John Kimball warmly and winsomely – without guilt – draws us to be wide-awake to the ministry opportunities available to us every day, all week long. An abundance of Scripture supports his thesis that low hanging fruit is everywhere and the Holy Spirit can empower all Christians to build redemptive relationships for the great good of people as well as to the glory of God. Read this book!"

 Dr. Pete Alwinson, FORGE, Orlando, FL

*John Kimball's latest book **Low Hanging Fruit** will challenge, encourage & equip you to realize more of your God-given identity, capacity and destiny. Prayerfully process the practical teaching contained within this timely Kingdom resource & you will experience a deeper empowerment from the Holy Spirit that will enable you to effectively move outward on mission with Master Jesus.*

John's passionate & demonstrated commitment to raise up and release Gospel centered, Spirit filled, & joy fueled missionary practitioners nearly leaps off every page. Take up and read! You will be glad you did.

 Foye Belyea, CEO, WarriorPriest Leadership Development Group; Co-founder, Anam Cara Life Community

"If you ever thought, 'There must be more to this Christian life than going to church,' or that 'Jesus' agonizing death must bring about more than an hour in church once a week,' then this book is for you. John Kimball describes this life of faith actually lived out intentionally with purpose. Following the Christian life described in this book requires trusting and submitting to the Holy Spirit, which is why relatively few live this way. But you can live this way trusting the Holy Spirit, and you will find that there is, indeed much more to this Christian life."

 Rev. Dr. Raymond DeLaurier, North Central Regional Pastor, Conservative Congregational Christian Conference

"Realism, inspiration and resource come together excellently for your equipping and mine. John Kimball's concept of low-hanging fruit is compellingly developed, with winsome prose and lots of Holy Spirit fire! John's writing locates this kingdom-shaped invitation in the undeniable relational heartland of the Trinity. Significant bible passages and essential ideas are very helpfully explored in responding to the beauty of Jesus. My prayer is that this resources a revolution of 'love and obedience all-day, everywhere!'"

Rev. Johnny Douglas, Vicar and Team Leader, St Peter's Church Hextable & St Paul's Church Swanley Village England

"It's apparent that the Lord has led John Kimball to write this volume 'for such a time as this'! Packed with readily understandable examples from the Scriptures, as you read and apply this teaching about the concept of low-hanging fruit you will be motivated toward more faithful obedience in bearing much fruit in the 'ripe harvest' for Jesus' kingdom. I have been encouraged and reenergized to this end!"

Rev. Dave Eisley, Pastor, Allenville Baptist Church, Allenville WI

"Pastor John believes it, he teaches it, and he lives out exactly what he writes in this book. I know because I once was one of his low-hanging fruits. He came alongside me as I accepted Christ and then accepted my calling to become a missionary. He didn't just tell me what to do, he demonstrated everything he describes, becoming a partner with the Holy Spirit leading the way. In this book, he lays out step by step how important building redemptive relationships is and makes it easy to follow and understand. I love how he uses scripture to back up scripture, then shares the Holy Spirit's role in this process. I have also had my own low-hanging fruit and made this a part of my ministry, and you can too."

Toni McAndrew, Missionary and Teacher of The Deaf, San Salvador, El Salvador

"John Kimball has written a book about low-hanging fruit that is filled with low-hanging Truth ripe for the harvesting! These Gospel truths are packaged and ready to influence your ministry, your relationships, and even to challenge your own heart. No need to spend countless hours searching it out - Kimball presents it clearly, concisely, and completely, even including the scriptural passages, so the reader does not have to stop to look them up in a separate volume. As I read, I found my own heart and mind filled with a renewed desire to pay attention for opportunities to share the truth of the gospel with the people God has already brought and will continue to bring across my path."

    Rev. Susan E. Moody, Interim Pastor and Recording Secretary of the Conservative Congregational Christian Conference

"John Kimball has created an excellent publication for practical evangelism and building discipleship. It's impossible to do it except through the work of the Holy Spirit. He guides us through His promptings to gather low hanging fruit that exists already within our daily environment. Beginning in Acts 2 John uses many scriptures as illustrations to show how to prepare ourselves within the body of the local church to live out of our identity in Christ by loving and ministering to people the way Christ did as well as many of his Disciples.

"He summarizes it well himself with these words, 'Like the early church, we must be fully devoted to apostolic teaching, to the fellowship of believers, to life-on-life intimacy with each other, and to all facets of praying. We need to learn and practice faithful obedience — it takes time, like developing a set of muscles. We need to look for 'low hanging fruit' as we go through our everyday lives. We can expect that the people on whom the Holy Spirit is working will often open the door to us in conversation. We need to learn how to start spiritual conversations to triage where people are with Jesus. And then we need to purpose to make the most of every opportunity the Holy Spirit gives us, acting on the authority we have as Christ's ambassadors and relying on God to do what we cannot. We love, we speak, and we pray -- and then we leave the results up to Him.'"

    Dr. T. A. Powell, Online Adjunct Professor of Divinity at Liberty University, Lynchburg VA and Regent University, Virginia Beach VA

"Dr. John Kimball writes in a down to earth, understandable way. This book is deep, but is written in such a way that the average church member can understand it and glean great tools to reach low hanging fruit people in their lives to make a Kingdom Impact. Pastor Kimball takes us back to an issue that many in the church are scared to discuss on such a level as he does – The Holy Spirit.

"He writes, 'Let the Holy Spirit speak to you about the relationships you might already have where He has been working.' Not only do Christians sitting in the pews in the U.S. need to read this book, but it needs to be placed in the hands of missionaries around the world. It can help serve as a reminder to them that the Holy Spirit is working in the hearts and lives of those around them to prepare them to hear the Gospel and respond. May this book be used in churches and on the mission field to help people identify 'The Low Hanging Fruit' in their lives."

Jon Rissmiller, Missionary Care Specialist, Global Outreach International, Tupelo MS

"Jesus tells us that the fields are ripe for harvest! Do you believe Him? Pastor John Kimball does, and in his book, **Low Hanging Fruit**, he has given the 21st Century church a primer for how to join Jesus in His mission of making more disciples. Do you want to see God use you to find, reach, and disciple those who are ready to respond to the Gospel? If so, your time would be well spent in this book. Saturated with Scripture, real-life stories of transformation, with practical wisdom gained in over 35 years of vocational ministry, John Kimball writes as a disciple of Jesus who is passionate about making more disciples. I've seen John minister up close and personal and watched him from afar. He is the real deal! This book would be great for individual or group study. I recommend it wholeheartedly and am excited to see how God uses it to advance His Kingdom here, near and far."

Brian Schulenburg, Discipleship Pastor, Wooddale Church, Eden Prairie, MN

"A source of instruction and encouragement to both the young and mature believer. Written in such a way to motivate a look inside the heart and attitude for the follower of Christ who desires to make a difference and influence others."

Linda B. Vaughan, Executive Director, Emeritus, Union Mission Ministries, Norfolk VA

"'Besides, success is not up to you, it's up to the Holy Spirit. Take a deep breath and step out in faith.' These words from John Kimball's new book, **Low Hanging Fruit***, are just a few of the heart-gripping, life-inspection challenges given. This book brings a real, personal, and practical look at how the Church can expect 'real-life' to be lived out. Thank you, brother!"*

Rev. Dean Walker, Pastor, Garfield Christian Fellowship, Garfield WA

LOW HANGING FRUIT

LOW HANGING FRUIT

Partnering with the Holy Spirit for Greater Ministry Impact

John Kimball

LOW HANGING FRUIT
Partnering with the Holy Spirit for Greater Ministry Impact

© 2022 John R. Kimball

ISBN: 979-89858-423-0-2

No part of this book may be used or reproduced, stored in a retrieval system, or transmitted in any form or by any means — electronic, mechanical, photocopy, recording, or any other manner — without prior written permission from the author, except in case of brief quotations embodied in critical articles and reviews.

Scripture quotations taken from THE HOLY BIBLE: NEW LIVING TRANSLATION® NLT® Copyright © 2015 by Tyndale House Publishers. Used with permission. All rights reserved worldwide.

Design, Layout and Format by Kim Gardell

Published in the United States of America by
The Beaumeadow Group
Oviedo, Florida

DEDICATION

This book is dedicated to my precious congregation,
the Palmwood Church family,
who continue to bless me daily with their enthusiasm at learning and
carrying out the principles taught herein.

ACKNOWLEDGEMENTS

This book was many years in the making. What began as a conversation and then morphed into a Sunday message series, has now gained a much greater reach for Jesus' kingdom. I'm amazed at how God brought all the pieces together – and how many people have contributed to its success in some way, or urged me in its completion.

First and foremost, I would like to thank my family – and especially my bride of 33 years, Kathryn. Kathryn has been at my side in ministry since before we were married. She is more than a companion, she is a minister in her own right and has also been a kingdom warrior on occasion. I would have very little success in any area of ministry without her. And we're blessed that all of our kids (now adults) are living for Jesus and, in their own ways, are applying the principles laid out in this text.

I have been in the ministry 35 years and have learned many of these lessons "on the job," as I helped the congregations I have served to master the making of disciples. I have also been blessed to have a role in assisting many other churches nationally through the two other ministries under which I serve, my denomination, the Conservative Congregational Christian Conference (www.ccccusa.com) and the Praxis Center for Church Development (www.praxiscenter.org). But the most significant laboratory for what I teach here has been among the great folks of the Palmwood Church Family. I've had the distinct pleasure of planting and then pastoring this awesome band of believers. From our beginning, we have been putting these "low hanging fruit" principles in place and, as we master them more and more, we are clearly seeing their fruitfulness. I am grateful for my leadership team, Bob and Gayle Buford, Stephen O'Guin and Danny Eshcol, as they co-lead, partner with, and challenge me. These years have been both the most fruitful and enjoyable of my career in large part because of them.

I am grateful for the ongoing investment of several key brothers in Christ who come from very different backgrounds but who demonstrate how we balance and complement each other for a significantly greater kingdom impact. Father Jon Davis, Bishop Jayson Quiñones, Michael Brinkley, Steven Barr and Foye Belyea are all such sources of life and laughter. And each lives out what I teach in this book in very effective ways. I am also blessed to lead a national team in my denominational role who are committed to helping local churches across the country thrive in authentic kingdom ministry. Dave Eisley, Dave Balicki, Dean Walker, Dan Peterson, Matt Schraeder, Peter Wood, Scott Nice and Todd Venman are all strong and fruitful partners in this work who continue to have an "iron sharpens iron" impact in my life and ministry.

I have three men, in particular, who continue to disciple, coach and mentor me, and have each made a profound contribution to my learning on the topic of making disciples. Tom Johnston took me on as a disciple several years ago (I'm not sure he knew what he was in for!) and has brought incredible alignment in my life and ministry to the Kingdom of God. Mike Chong Perkinson, likewise, and he also served as my church planting coach in the early years of launching Palmwood Church. And Ron Hamilton, who has been a friend longer than I can remember and my boss (in my denominational role) for the last decade. I am so grateful for their ongoing investment of wisdom and expertise in my life.

I want to thank all those who reviewed the original manuscript of this book to make sure it was theologically sound and ready for publication. Some I've already mentioned helped with that task. In addition, I'd like to thank Ray DeLaurier for his insightful comments and contribution to the final work. I'd also like to thank my daughter, Lauren, for proofreading my manuscript, helping me get it ready for the process of publication.

Acknowledgements

Finally, I want to thank Kim Gardell, a dear friend and an incredible graphic artist, for taking the manuscript I gave her and making it both beautiful and ready for publication. Not many people are blessed with their own personal "typesetter!" She has gone above and beyond on this one.

It is my prayer that the book you now hold in your hand (or on your tablet) will be more than just a "good read." I hope that it forever changes the way you see the people around you. May Jesus' kingdom expand as a result.

TABLE OF CONTENTS

DEDICATION ix

ACKNOWLEDGEMENTS xi

INTRODUCTION... xvii

PART ONE– UNDERSTANDING LOW HANGING FRUIT

CHAPTER 1 1
Preparing Ourselves for the Task

CHAPTER 2 17
New Testament Examples

PART TWO– BUILDING REDEMPTIVE RELATIONSHIPS

CHAPTER 3 33
Building Redemptive Relationships (Part 1)

CHAPTER 4 45
Building Redemptive Relationships (Part 2)

PART THREE– CONNECTING WITH LOW HANGING FRUIT PEOPLE

CHAPTER 5 63
Praying With People

CHAPTER 6 77
Starting Spiritual Conversations

CHAPTER 7 87
Showing Jesus' Love

CHAPTER 8 99
Evangelizing People

CHAPTER 9 109
Memorizing Scripture Together

CHAPTER 10 119
Real Fellowship

CHAPTER 11 131
Final Thoughts

OTHER BOOKS BY JOHN KIMBALL *135*

INTRODUCTION

You know the saying, 'Four months between planting and harvest.' But I say, wake up and look around. The fields are already ripe for harvest.
(John 4:35, New Living Translation)

He said to his disciples, "The harvest is great, but the workers are few. So pray to the Lord who is in charge of the harvest; ask him to send more workers into his fields."
(Matthew 9:37-38, New Living Translation)

Our world is in upheaval. Surveys like those done by Pew Research[1] proclaim that the percentage of the population attending church in the United States is lower than ever before and is dwindling. Politics, social issues and other factors have helped make Christianity unpopular in North America among those who see its followers as unsophisticated, intolerant and even mean. The ministry and witness of Jesus' Church is tough and resistance seems very high. Christians are more apprehensive than ever to talk about their faith. All these things are true.

But what if I were to tell you that Scriptures like those above are also true? What if I were to tell you that they may be more true in our world today

---

1 In U.S., Decline of Christianity Continues at Rapid Pace, Pew Research Center (pewforum.org), online. 17 October 2019.

than at any other time in our lifetimes? What if I could promise you that you could have a more fruitful witness for Jesus *in today's world* than you've ever had before? Would you believe me?

Precisely because of all the challenges of the last few years, the harvest fields of human hearts around us are ripe. People are looking for answers - strength, security and healing. And the Holy Spirit has never stopped his work on such hearts, using life's circumstances to prepare them to receive the seed of God's Word as "good soil" (Luke 8:4-15). It's when we partner with what he is already doing in those hearts that we can see a great spiritual return on our investment into people for Jesus' kingdom and glory.

I have become convinced that we Christians, particularly in the West, make our witness and ministry a lot more difficult than it needs to be. All ministry has its challenges, to be sure. But we often add unnecessary travail. I remember talking with one friend who told me of her frustration in witnessing to her sister. For the last several years, every time the subject of religion came up, she would try to woo her sister to Jesus. She was kind. She was not particularly overbearing. And yet, her sister often reacted with frustration. When she talked to me about it, she was surprised when I said, "Sounds like you're trying to convert someone that the Holy Spirit has not yet made ready." She paused. Then she asked me to tell her more. That conversation ultimately turned into a Sunday message series, and now into the book you hold in your hands.

In June of 1976, a Southern Baptist pastor named Henry Blackaby started a wonderful world-wide movement when he began teaching people to stop just doing things for God and, instead, to look to see where God is working around them and join what he is already doing. That teaching grew and would become the landmark Bible study series, *Experiencing God: Knowing and Doing the Will of God*.[2] That biblical principle is critical to keep in mind for all areas of life, ministry and witness.

When it comes to sharing Christ, we often feel burdened to "do more." And yet most Christians also have an unspoken fear that all their efforts will be fruitless. Some have been diligent in trying, but they've seen precious

---

[2] Blackaby, Henry, *Experiencing God: Knowing and Doing the Will of God*, Nashville: LifeWay Christian Resources, 2009. (You can see the whole line of *Experiencing God* products on the LifeWay website. Experiencing God | Lifeway.)

Introduction

few results. But I submit to you that, if we were to take Blackaby's advice, we might start seeing what I call "Low Hanging Fruit" all around us. Let me explain.

I am blessed to live in Central Florida. I have several kinds of citrus trees in my garden — a mature Ruby Red Grapefruit tree, a mature Oro Blanco Grapefruit tree, an abundant Meyer Lemon that fruits 6 months of the year, and a young Valencia Orange tree that is just starting to really produce. Each of these trees begins fruiting at a different time. We are able to enjoy delicious, tree-ripened fruit for several months each year. When the fruit of a tree is ready, I don't go and get my 9-foot ladder and start pulling the fruit from the top of the tree. I begin with the ripe fruit that is on the lower branches within reach that just fall off in my hand. Like everyone else in my neighborhood, I start with the low hanging fruit. It's the quickest and easiest part of the harvest. More than once I have reached higher to pick fruit that was not yet ripe — you can yank it hard and force it off the branch, but you'll regret it when you try to eat it. It's hard to pick — its skin is tough — and its flesh is bitter. There's nothing like tree-ripened fruit that is ready to eat.

Too often I think we Christians decide for ourselves who we will "target" with the gospel and other forms of ministry. And in many cases, I think we're getting out the proverbial 9-foot ladder, going after fruit that is not yet ripe. Witnessing to these people is much more difficult. They are resistant. They have tough "skin" when it comes to the Word of God and explaining the gospel. And they are often bitter that we keep pursuing them. But when we partner with what the Holy Spirit is already doing in the lives of those around us, prayerfully paying attention to those who are becoming responsive in other areas of ministry, our witness for Christ is more fruitful and, many times, easier.

This book is written for those who want to see more fruit in their walk with Jesus. It's not just about evangelism, but about our witness in all areas of ministry. It has been my experience, as both a Christian and as a pastor, that taking the time to see what the Holy Spirit is already doing makes a huge difference in my own spiritual yield. My prayer is that the following pages bless you with a new perspective, yes. But even moreso, a renewed passion to get out into our world — turbulent as it is — and invest with the Spirit into many people's lives. We won't always get it right; however, when we spend more time looking to see where the Holy Spirit is already working, we will all see more fruit.

May God bless you with abundant and sweet "low hanging fruit"!

—John Kimball
Oviedo, Florida
May 2021

PART ONE

Understanding Low Hanging Fruit

CHAPTER 1
Preparing Ourselves for the Task

All the believers devoted themselves to the apostles' teaching, and to fellowship, and to sharing in meals (including the Lord's Supper), and to prayer.

A deep sense of awe came over them all, and the apostles performed many miraculous signs and wonders. And all the believers met together in one place and shared everything they had. They sold their property and possessions and shared the money with those in need. They worshiped together at the Temple each day, met in homes for the Lord's Supper, and shared their meals with great joy and generosity—all the while praising God and enjoying the goodwill of all the people. And each day the Lord added to their fellowship those who were being saved (Acts 2:42-47, New Living Translation).

The sad reality about today's North American Church at large is that we have stopped consistently practicing the things that connect us most with our God. We don't pray as we should anymore. We don't read the Bible, let alone study and apply it, as we should anymore. And we don't make disciples like we should anymore. By foregoing things like these, we also make it increasingly more difficult to see what the Holy Spirit is doing around us. We render ourselves ineffective for the cause of

Christ. But it doesn't have to stay that way! In this chapter, I hope to lay a foundation for us upon which we can build the practical ideas in the rest of this book — practical actions we can take to consistently partner with the Holy Spirit in our everyday lives.

In the days and weeks after the Holy Spirit birthed the Church at Pentecost (Acts 2) those early Christians passionately lived out the realities of their faith, and their impact was enormous. They provide a wonderful roadmap for us. A great example is the encounter of Peter and John with a desperate beggar at the Temple's Beautiful Gate.

> *Peter and John went to the Temple one afternoon to take part in the three o'clock prayer service. As they approached the Temple, a man lame from birth was being carried in. Each day he was put beside the Temple gate, the one called the Beautiful Gate, so he could beg from the people going into the Temple. When he saw Peter and John about to enter, he asked them for some money.*
>
> *Peter and John looked at him intently, and Peter said, "Look at us!" The lame man looked at them eagerly, expecting some money. But Peter said, "I don't have any silver or gold for you. But I'll give you what I have. In the name of Jesus Christ the Nazarene, get up and walk!"*
>
> *Then Peter took the lame man by the right hand and helped him up. And as he did, the man's feet and ankles were instantly healed and strengthened. He jumped up, stood on his feet, and began to walk! Then, walking, leaping, and praising God, he went into the Temple with them.*
>
> *All the people saw him walking and heard him praising God. When they realized he was the lame beggar they had seen so often at the Beautiful Gate, they were absolutely astounded! They all rushed out in amazement to Solomon's Colonnade, where the man was holding tightly to Peter and John* (Acts 3:1-11, New Living Translation).

There are several things we can learn from this story.

Peter and John were Already Prepared

This story in Acts 3 must be taken in the context of the Jesus-centered, Spirit-empowered, gospel-directed life described in Acts 2. According to Acts 2:42, the apostles and members of the early church were fully devoted to four things that aligned them with the heart of God and empowered them for their mission. These four things helped them remain vitally "tuned in" to the work of the Holy Spirit all around them.

Apostolic Teaching. They were consistently immersing themselves into the teaching of the apostles. This was the teaching and guidance of those who had ministered with Jesus. These men had learned from the Lord himself as he tutored them in the scriptures (what we would now call the Old Testament — the Law of Moses, the prophets and the writings). We know that Jesus spent his time explaining from all the scriptures the things concerning himself (Luke 24:27). These men then uniquely saw the unfolding of the plan of God for humanity's redemption. They saw how Jesus embodied the kingdom of God. They understood the pivotal impact of the cross. And they now passed all this onto the rest of the church.

The Fellowship of Believers. They were in regular communion with the growing number of brothers and sisters in Christ. This communion included the teaching, but also living life together, worship and serving others. It's important to note that what many people think is fellowship today is not really what was happening in the early church. Fellowship for them was not just meeting together and enjoying each other's company. It was "relationship with a reason." Living life with one another, they were literally on mission together. My friend Tom Johnston describes it as "...the shared life together in Christ of a group of disciples who have a regular, consistent devotion to participating in and with each other in an organic life/ministry holism."[3]

There is another key point to be made, this was a devotion to the whole body of Christ, not just select individuals. In many English versions of the Bible, this part of Acts 2:42 is translated "...to fellowship..." But in the Greek, there is a definite article before the word *koinonia* (fellowship). It is devotion to *the* fellowship. This is the kind and quality of familial love and devotion Christ commanded his followers to have when he said,

---

[3] Johnston, Tom. *The Way of the Master: The Leader Development Methodology of Jesus* (p. 14). Kindle Edition.

> *"So now I am giving you a new commandment: Love each other. Just as I have loved you, you should love each other. Your love for one another will prove to the world that you are my disciples"* (John 13:34-45, New Living Translation).

They had this kind of devotion to the fellowship of believers, which leads to the next key component.

The Breaking of Bread. They ate together. Most people assume this is a reference to communion. I am sure it included celebrating The Lord's Table together because we know it was a regular observance (see Acts 20:7-12). But the language here is different. I believe it is a reference to communal meals. They ate regular family meals together because they were devoted to each other (Acts 2:46).

Never was this point made more clear to me than when I was on a ministry trip to Israel. One afternoon during our visit, our host had us all pile in a van and drive to a local restaurant for lunch. I had the pleasure of sitting next to a Jewish brother in Christ during our meal. As we were finishing the food, he noted, "You know, there is something I find American Christians do not understand about our Jewish culture." Truly interested, I asked him to explain. "Let me put it this way. If a Jew such as myself says to you, 'Let's go to this restaurant and eat,' it means he is hungry. But if that same Jew said, 'Tonight, come to my home and have supper with my wife, my children and me,' it means you are *family*." All of a sudden Acts 2 made perfect sense! In the early church culture, there were few things more intimate for the believers than sharing a meal together. They were devoted to the breaking of bread.

Prayer. The early Christians were devoted to prayer. I believe this is the full gamut of prayer as described by the apostle Paul to his son-in-the-faith, Timothy:

> *"I urge you, first of all, to pray for all people. Ask God to help them; intercede on their behalf, and give thanks for them. Pray this way for kings and all who are in authority so that we can live peaceful and quiet lives marked by godliness and dignity. This is good and pleases God our Savior, who wants everyone to be saved and to understand the truth."* (1 Timothy 2:1, New Living Translation)

Paul uses four different Greek terms here, essentially giving four kinds of prayer:

1. Prayers (*proseuchē*) - these are our regular, ongoing conversation with God like our devotions and quick prayers as you think of things throughout the day.

2. Ask for help (*deēsis*) - these are requests, often urgent supplication or pleas for God to intervene in someone's life or circumstances.[4]

3. Intercede on their behalf (*enteuxis*) - this is true intercession or "stand in the gap" prayer, which I define as praying for the will of God to come to full fruition in someone's life or in a community.

4. Give thanks for them (*eucharista*) - this is giving God praise and gratitude for both those for whom we are praying and what he is doing in their lives.

When Luke (the author of Acts) says the early Christians were devoted to prayer, I believe he means all four of these together.

Peter and John were already prepared for encounters like the one with this desperate beggar at the Temple because they were devoted to these things. Further, they were in regular fellowship with a growing community of people who were also devoted to these things. They did not have to guess what the Holy Spirit was doing with that beggar. They were in such regular communion with the Spirit in and through the early church community that they could already tell he was working.

Peter and John had Practiced Praying for the Sick

Anyone who has played an instrument or a sport knows the saying, "Practice makes perfect." If you want to become really good at anything, you have to do it over and over again. We make mistakes, but we learn

---

4   In the Greek New Testament, *deēsis* comes first in the sequence. The New Living Translation reverses the order of the first two kinds of prayer in this passage.

from them. We build "muscle memory." We may even learn new techniques that help us master what we're practicing. Peter and John were already doing this when they met the beggar.

While Jesus was still alive, he sent his apostles out to practice what he had been teaching them. In Matthew 10 we read that

> *Jesus sent out the twelve apostles with these instructions: "Don't go to the Gentiles or the Samaritans, but only to the people of Israel— God's lost sheep. Go and announce to them that the Kingdom of Heaven is near. Heal the sick, raise the dead, cure those with leprosy, and cast out demons. Give as freely as you have received!* (Matthew 10:5ff, New Living Translation)

This was only the beginning. Throughout the remainder of their time with Jesus, he would teach them and then challenge them to apply what they were learning. They got lots of practice.

By the time we get to Acts 3 — after Jesus' ascension and the outpouring of the Holy Spirit to birth the church — Peter and John are likely now mastering prayer and intercession. They've seen God work all kinds of miracles in response to prayer. They don't just have an academic understanding of prayer principles, they have real experience with both how to pray and wisdom to know the kind of results they should expect. It was a regular part of life.

Peter and John were About Their Normal Routine

Notice that Peter and John were not doing anything "special" when they met the desperate beggar. They were on their way to the Temple to take part in the afternoon prayer service. We're told in Acts 2:46 that they worshipped in the Temple every day. They were just going about their normal, daily routine. But there's more.

Notice that the beggar was also going about his normal, daily routine!

> *"As they approached the Temple, a man lame from birth was being carried in. Each day he was put beside the Temple gate, the one called the Beautiful Gate, so he could beg from the people going into the Temple"* (Acts 3:2, New Living Translation).

The only thing special about the encounter between Peter, John and the beggar was The Holy Spirit! Everyone was simply going about their normal day.

This is a critical thing. Seeing the Holy Spirit working around us should be a normal, everyday occurrence. Jesus' people are always on mission. In fact, the Great Commission actually instructs us to be. As Jesus is preparing to ascend on the cloud of God's glory, he raises his hands to rabbinically bless his followers and gives them this parting commission:

> *"I have been given all authority in heaven and on earth. Therefore, go and make disciples of all the nations, baptizing them in the name of the Father and the Son and the Holy Spirit. Teach these new disciples to obey all the commands I have given you. And be sure of this: I am with you always, even to the end of the age"* (Matthew 28:18-20, New Living Translation).

Jesus' commissioning "Therefore, go…" is actually a participial phrase. Where "make disciples," "baptize" and "teach" are all imperatives, one could argue that "go" is different. A participle is like our English words ending in "ing." A better translation might be "Therefore, going, make disciples" or "As you are going, make disciples." *As you are going.* At least in part the language tells us that the Commission is to be always engaged. As we are going, we make disciples. As we go about our daily lives, we make disciples. It's to be a normal, everyday part of life.

The Beggar Invited the Encounter

This is the essence of "low hanging fruit"! How many times did Peter and John come that way in their daily prayer routine? How many times had they seen this desperate beggar? How many times had he seen them? It was the beggar that initiated the conversation, asking Peter and John for money (Acts 3:3). This scenario is actually quite common! The Holy

Spirit orchestrates things and we simply have to be observant. It's not at all unusual for the person we're calling "low hanging fruit" to open the door for an initial conversation and more.

I cannot tell you how many times the most incredible, Spirit-led encounters have happened just like this. Someone in line in a coffee shop notices the cross on my seminary ring and asks about it, making religious small talk as the Holy Spirit whispers to my heart, "Pay attention!" An exasperated young mom at one of our many Orlando theme parks is ready to call it a day and "randomly" asks if I have any grandkids. The Holy Spirit whispers, "Pray with her." A person who is considered completely unreachable experiences the loss of a loved one and is devastated, turning to me out of desperation and becomes instantly inquisitive about the afterlife. The Holy Spirit says, "Just be quiet and let her lead the conversation." And in each case, heaven moves on earth and these precious souls have an encounter with my Jesus because I'm simply paying attention.

Peter and John Respond with What They Have to Offer

Led by the Holy Spirit, Peter turns the conversation with the beggar in a spiritual direction (we have a whole chapter devoted to that!). In this case, it was short and to the point — but it's not always that way. Peter accepted the invitation into this man's life and turned the encounter toward Jesus.

In many cases, the spiritual conversation will actually be the whole encounter early on. This beggar responded quickly, but not everyone is that ready. The key is to be sensitive to the leading of the Spirit throughout. The Holy Spirit will nudge you to take it deeper. The Holy Spirit will also sometimes lead you to hold your tongue. Learn to follow his lead because he is the one preparing the heart of the person in your encounter. He knows things you do not. You may simply be planting a seed that he will have someone else water at a later time.

Peter Spoke with His God-given Authority

This authority is real — but many North American Christians either do not know it or they do not really believe it. When the apostle John says, "Greater is the One who is in you than the one who lives in the world" (1 John 4:4), he means it. This is so important that I need to take an aside to explain it.

God's authority was shared in the Garden of Eden. Humanity was made in the image and likeness of God.

> *Then God said, "Let us make human beings in our image, to be like us. They will reign over the fish in the sea, the birds in the sky, the livestock, all the wild animals on the earth, and the small animals that scurry along the ground."*
>
> *So God created human beings in his own image.*
>
> *In the image of God he created them;*
>
> *male and female he created them.*
>
> *Then God blessed them and said, "Be fruitful and multiply. Fill the earth and govern it. Reign over the fish in the sea, the birds in the sky, and all the animals that scurry along the ground"* (Genesis 1:26-28, New Living Translation).

Wayne Grudem says the Hebrew terminology used for "image" and "like us" are best expressed, "Let us make human beings to be like us and to represent us."[5] Humanity was to represent God from the beginning and to *rule* as his regents on the earth. We were to complete the work he had begun. All the earth was "very good" (Genesis 1:31), but outside of Eden it was still wild and needed to be brought under submission. The word "govern" above is the Hebrew word *kabash*, meaning to subdue, dominate or bring into bondage. God gave us full authority over creation to subdue it and to rule it on his behalf.

Man gave that shared authority away to Satan the usurper. Everything was perfect until Genesis Chapter 3. The serpent, Satan, tempted our first parents, the federal heads of humanity. Many wonder why this is such a big deal — everyone is tempted. But it was not the temptation itself that was sinful. It was their decision to give in.

A little more theology here is helpful. There is a Latin phrase that explains it best: *posse non pecare*. It means "power not to sin." Remember, the first man and woman were very good by God's own standard — himself (Genesis 1:31). They were perfect. They were exactly as he designed them

---

5   Grudem, Wayne, *Systematic Theology: An Introduction to Biblical Doctrine,* Grand Rapids: Zondervan, 1994. The Doctrine of Man.

to be. And this means that they had absolutely no predisposition to sin. Read that again. They were not tainted by sin at all. This means that, unlike us, temptation had no real power over them. For the rest of us, there is always a level of temptation where we will cave in. But not the first humans. They did not experience temptation's draw as we do. That's what makes their decision to surrender to Satan so heinous. And even if one thinks Satan pulled a fast one by going to Eve, who got God's command second-hand, the reality is Adam was standing right there all along and did not administer his God-given authority over the usurper. Yes, you read that right. He was there all along and said nothing.

> *"The woman was convinced. She saw that the tree was beautiful and its fruit looked delicious, and she wanted the wisdom it would give her. So she took some of the fruit and ate it. Then she gave some to her husband, **who was with her**, and he ate it, too* (Genesis 3:6, New Living Translation, **emphasis mine**).

You see, living in a perfect state of *posse non pecare* means that they *decided* to surrender to Satan. He didn't pull any wool over their eyes. They *chose* to do it. And that choice was costly — to all humanity for all time. The Latin designation changed from that point forward to *non posse non pecare* or "no power not to sin." Humanity was sunk. And what's worse, as God's regents over creation, the act of surrender handed over their authority to the Deceiver.

Satan holds that authority throughout the Bible narrative. Satan grabbed the keys to creation, as it were. And he has wreaked havoc ever since. What God created as good became tainted through and through with evil. What was sacred (set apart) became common. What was glorious became putrid. What was perfect became broken, bent, destroyed. And humanity no longer had the power to stop the degradation on God's behalf.

Satan took charge of the earth. The Scripture shows us this:

- Satan patrols the earth, watching over it. *"One day the members of the heavenly court came to present themselves before the Lord, and the Accuser, Satan, came with them. "Where have you come* from?" the Lord asked Satan. Satan answered the Lord, "I have been patrolling the earth, watching everything that's going on" (Job 1:6-7, New Living Translation).

- Peter says he prowls around like a hungry lion. *"Stay alert! Watch out for your great enemy, the devil. He prowls around like a roaring lion, looking for someone to devour* (1 Peter 5:8, New Living Translation).
- Paul refers to him as the "god of this world." *"Satan, who is the god of this world, has blinded the minds of those who don't believe. They are unable to see the glorious light of the Good News. They don't understand this message about the glory of Christ, who is the exact likeness of God"* (2 Corinthians 4:4, New Living Translation).
- Paul also says that he commands the disobedient. *"You used to live in sin, just like the rest of the world, obeying the devil—the commander of the powers in the unseen world"* (Ephesians 2:2).
- John says he has power over the whole earth. *"We know that we are children of God and that the world around us is under the control of the evil one"* (1 John 5:19, New Living Translation).
- Jesus calls him the ruler of this world; but notes that He will defeat him. *"The time for judging this world has come, when Satan, the ruler of this world, will be cast out. And when I am lifted up from the earth, I will draw everyone to myself"* (John 12:31-32, New Living Translation; see also John 14:30 and John 16:11).

The point is, when the first humans surrendered themselves to Satan, they gave away their God-given authority to subdue creation and to rule over it. The Devil took full advantage.

Jesus takes the authority back. Here's the good news. Jesus begins the deputation proclamation of the Great Commission with these words: "I have been given all authority in heaven and on earth..." (Matthew 28:18, New Living Translation). Did you catch that? ALL authority. Where? In heaven AND ON EARTH! When Jesus defeated Satan on the cross of Calvary, *He took back the authority from the usurper!* Jesus took the authority back! He now has all authority both in heaven and in all creation!

And what does he do with it? HE GIVES IT BACK TO US! The Great Commission is a great reset, restoring Jesus' redeemed followers back to their place of God-shared authority. The difference is that now, via the gospel, the mission includes redemption and reconciliation as our King uses us to *subdue* the kingdom of darkness and its effects, setting captives free on his behalf.

> *Jesus came and told his disciples, "I have been given all authority in heaven and on earth. Therefore, go and make disciples of all the nations, baptizing them in the name of the Father and the Son and the Holy Spirit. Teach these new disciples to obey all the commands I have given you. And be sure of this: I am with you always, even to the end of the age."* (Matthew 28:18-20, New Living Translation).

God's shared authority with his human regents. God gave it to us. We gave it up. Satan usurped it. Satan reigned with it. Jesus defeated Satan. Jesus took it back. And then Jesus turned around and shared it again. This blows my mind!

We are Christ's ambassadors. Christian, did you know that you are a fully deputized ambassador of the King of all kings and the Lord of all lords? If you have surrendered to Jesus as Savior and Lord, then you are already his ambassador. It was set up at the cross. It was ratified in the Great Commission. Paul even calls us all ambassadors. Look at this second letter to the Christians at Corinth.

> *Because we understand our fearful responsibility to the Lord, we work hard to persuade others. God knows we are sincere, and I hope you know this, too. Are we commending ourselves to you again? No, we are giving you a reason to be proud of us, so you can answer those who brag about having a spectacular ministry rather than having a sincere heart. If it seems we are crazy, it is to bring glory to God. And if we are in our right minds, it is for your benefit. Either way, Christ's love controls us. Since we believe that Christ died for all, we also believe that we have all died to our old life. He died for everyone so that those who receive his new life will no longer live for themselves. Instead, they will live for Christ, who died and was raised for them.*

So we have stopped evaluating others from a human point of view. At one time we thought of Christ merely from a human point of view. How differently we know him now! This means that anyone who belongs to Christ has become a new person. The old life is gone; a new life has begun!

And all of this is a gift from God, who brought us back to himself through Christ. And God has given us this task of reconciling people to him. For God was in Christ, reconciling the world to himself, no longer counting people's sins against them. And he gave us this wonderful message of reconciliation. ***So we are Christ's ambassadors****; God is making his appeal through us. We speak for Christ when we plead, "Come back to God!" For God made Christ, who never sinned, to be the offering for our sin, so that we could be made right with God through Christ* (2 Corinthians 5:11-21, New Living Translation, **emphasis mine**).

What is an ambassador? It's an *authorized representative*. Almost sounds like we were made for this (think: "Let us make human beings to be like us and to represent us," Genesis 1:26). We are given Christ's authority (Great Commission) to represent him (ambassadors) and to complete his mission. What is his mission? Jesus himself tells us this in Luke 4:

When he came to the village of Nazareth, his boyhood home, he went as usual to the synagogue on the Sabbath and stood up to read the Scriptures. The scroll of Isaiah the prophet was handed to him. He unrolled the scroll and found the place where this was written:

"*The Spirit of the Lord is upon me,*

for he has anointed me to bring Good News to the poor.

He has sent me to proclaim that captives will be released,

that the blind will see,

that the oppressed will be set free,

and that the time of the Lord's favor has come."

> *He rolled up the scroll, handed it back to the attendant, and sat down. All eyes in the synagogue looked at him intently. Then he began to speak to them. "The Scripture you've just heard has been fulfilled this very day!"* (Luke 4:16-21, New Living Translation).

Jesus shared this mission with his apostles (Matthew 10:5-8). Jesus shared this mission later with Paul (Acts 26:15-18). And he shares this same mission with all those who follow him (Matthew 28:18-20; Mark 16:15-20; Acts 1:6-11). This brings us back to Peter, John and the beggar at the Temple gate.

Peter and John knew their God-given authority. Peter and John were already living out the various habits and practices that kept them connected to the whispers of the Holy Spirit. Peter and John knew the mission they were on. So when they passed the beggar on this particular day, they were ready for the encounter. In the authority of Jesus, and the power of the Holy Spirit, Peter spoke and then left the results up to God. And we must learn to do the same thing.

The Result

Peter and John were living a life of mission-preparedness with the rest of the believers in Jerusalem. As they lived their daily lives, they were ready and watching for any and every opportunity to fulfill the mission they had been given. And they understood the ambassadorial authority with which they had been endued. On the day they met the desperate beggar at the Temple's Beautiful Gate, they knew their place in the mosaic of things the Holy Spirit was orchestrating, and the result was a life-changing God-encounter for many. The beggar was healed, yes. And that in and of itself was huge. But there was also a Spirit-led ripple effect:

> *"Then Peter took the lame man by the right hand and helped him up. And as he did, the man's feet and ankles were instantly healed and strengthened. He jumped up, stood on his feet, and began to walk! Then, walking, leaping, and praising God, he went into the Temple with them.*
>
> *All the people saw him walking and heard him praising God. When they realized he was the lame beggar they had seen so often at the*

Beautiful Gate, they were absolutely astounded! They all rushed out in amazement to Solomon's Colonnade, where the man was holding tightly to Peter and John" (Acts 3:7-11, New Living Translation).

When we faithfully play our own unique roles in the wider, ongoing redemption plan of Jesus, partnering with the Holy Spirit wherever we see him at work or following his loving nudge, there will always be a ripple effect. I will never forget one particular encounter I had years ago. A daughter of someone in my church was dying of pancreatic cancer. I loved the family in my congregation, and they regularly pleaded with me to visit her and pray for her. The problem is that she was not having it. She was not a believer. In fact, she was an antagonist. There were many very rocky encounters as I tried to bring her the peace of Jesus. But then, one night I was awakened by a call at two o'clock in the morning. She had been rushed to the hospital with internal bleeding. Things looked dire. But this time I felt the peace of Christ as I got dressed and headed for my car. I prayed as I drove across town and felt something was happening. As I entered the ICU where she was recovering after emergency surgery, she called to me! Her heart had completely changed. That night she responded gloriously to the gospel — as did other family members sitting with her in the ICU bay! When the Holy Spirit orchestrates an encounter, it is not unusual for multiple people to be impacted by it.

Friends, being fully useful to the Holy Spirit requires preparation and readiness on our part. Like the early church, we must be fully devoted to apostolic teaching, to the fellowship of believers, to life-on-life intimacy with each other, and to all facets of praying. We need to learn and practice faithful obedience — it takes time, like developing a set of muscles. We need to look for "low hanging fruit" as we go through our everyday lives. We can expect that the people on whom the Holy Spirit is working will often open the door to us in conversation. We need to learn how to start spiritual conversations to triage where people are with Jesus. And then we need to purpose to make the most of every opportunity the Holy Spirit gives us, acting on the authority we have as Christ's ambassadors and relying on God to do what we cannot. We love, we speak and we pray — and then we leave the results up to Him.

Are you ready for a phenomenal adventure? Then read on! In the chapters that follow I will provide some New Testament examples to guide us and then I will outline some practical, everyday practices we can develop to grow in our partnership with the Holy Spirit. We'll talk about regularly praying with people, building redemptive relationships, how to start and steer spiritual conversations, consistently showing Jesus' love through a life of serving others, evangelizing people, memorizing scripture together, establishing real fellowship and fulfilling our mission through disciple-making relationships. My prayer is that you (and I) will never be the same.

CHAPTER 2
New Testament Examples

As for Philip, an angel of the Lord said to him, "Go south down the desert road that runs from Jerusalem to Gaza." So he started out, and he met the treasurer of Ethiopia, a eunuch of great authority under the Kandake, the queen of Ethiopia. The eunuch had gone to Jerusalem to worship, and he was now returning. Seated in his carriage, he was reading aloud from the book of the prophet Isaiah.

*The Holy Spirit said to Philip,
"Go over and walk along beside the carriage."*

Philip ran over and heard the man reading from the prophet Isaiah. Philip asked, "Do you understand what you are reading?"
(Acts 8:26-30, New Living Translation)

We need to live lives so attuned to the Holy Spirit, that we can act quickly and faithfully when he beckons us. Philip is a great example of this. An angel of the Lord gave him instructions, and he jumped right on it. Like Philip, we need to have a heart for what we're calling "low hanging fruit" people. When we talk about "low hanging fruit," we're not at all being derogatory. We're simply referring to those that the Holy Spirit has so influenced as to be ready to encounter the risen Jesus through your love, your ministry and even the gospel itself.

Jesus and "Low Hanging Fruit" People

The gospel accounts show us that Jesus did not heal every person with needs around him. He healed and delivered many, but not all. That said, everyone who came to him, and those to whom he was led, saw God work in miraculous ways. There are multiple examples of this in the four gospels. Let's look at some.

Jesus healed and delivered people who came to him from all over the region of Galilee.

> *Jesus traveled throughout the region of Galilee, teaching in the synagogues and announcing the Good News about the Kingdom. And he healed every kind of disease and illness. News about him spread as far as Syria, and people soon began bringing to him all who were sick. And whatever their sickness or disease, or if they were demon possessed or epileptic or paralyzed—he healed them all. Large crowds followed him wherever he went—people from Galilee, the Ten Towns, Jerusalem, from all over Judea, and from east of the Jordan River.* (Matthew 4:23-25, New Living Translation).

Jesus healed a man with leprosy — by *touching* him.

> *Large crowds followed Jesus as he came down the mountainside. Suddenly, a man with leprosy approached him and knelt before him. "Lord," the man said, "if you are willing, you can heal me and make me clean."*
>
> *Jesus reached out and touched him. "I am willing," he said. "Be healed!" And instantly the leprosy disappeared. Then Jesus said to him, "Don't tell anyone about this. Instead, go to the priest and let him examine you. Take along the offering required in the law of Moses for those who have been healed of leprosy. This will be a public testimony that you have been cleansed"* (Matthew 4:1-4, New Living Translation).

Jesus healed a paralytic brought to him by friends.

Some people brought to him a paralyzed man on a mat. Seeing their faith, Jesus said to the paralyzed man, "Be encouraged, my child! Your sins are forgiven."

But some of the teachers of religious law said to themselves, "That's blasphemy! Does he think he's God?"

Jesus knew what they were thinking, so he asked them, "Why do you have such evil thoughts in your hearts? Is it easier to say 'Your sins are forgiven,' or 'Stand up and walk'? So I will prove to you that the Son of Man has the authority on earth to forgive sins." Then Jesus turned to the paralyzed man and said, "Stand up, pick up your mat, and go home!"

And the man jumped up and went home! Fear swept through the crowd as they saw this happen. And they praised God for giving humans such authority (Matthew 9:2-8, New Living Translation).

Jesus healed a woman who had suffered with a menstrual issue for twelve years and raised a synagogue leader's daughter from the dead all on the same afternoon!

As Jesus was saying this, the leader of a synagogue came and knelt before him. "My daughter has just died," he said, "but you can bring her back to life again if you just come and lay your hand on her."

So Jesus and his disciples got up and went with him. Just then a woman who had suffered for twelve years with constant bleeding came up behind him. She touched the fringe of his robe, for she thought, "If I can just touch his robe, I will be healed."

Jesus turned around, and when he saw her he said, "Daughter, be encouraged! Your faith has made you well." And the woman was healed at that moment.

When Jesus arrived at the official's home, he saw the noisy crowd and heard the funeral music. "Get out!" he told them. "The girl isn't dead; she's only asleep." But the crowd laughed at him. After the crowd was put outside, however, Jesus went in and took the girl by the hand, and she stood up! The report of this miracle swept through the entire countryside (Matthew 9:18-26, New Living Translation).

Jesus healed a couple of blind men by the roadside.

> *As Jesus and the disciples left the town of Jericho, a large crowd followed behind. Two blind men were sitting beside the road. When they heard that Jesus was coming that way, they began shouting, "Lord, Son of David, have mercy on us!"*
>
> *"Be quiet!" the crowd yelled at them.*
>
> *But they only shouted louder, "Lord, Son of David, have mercy on us!"*
>
> *When Jesus heard them, he stopped and called, "What do you want me to do for you?"*
>
> *"Lord," they said, "we want to see!" Jesus felt sorry for them and touched their eyes. Instantly they could see! Then they followed him* (Matthew 20:29-34, New Living Translation).

Jesus responded to the faith of a hated Roman Centurion whose beloved servant was ill. This one is particularly fascinating because Jesus proclaims that he has not seen the depths of faith this Centurion displayed among all the people of Israel!

> *When Jesus returned to Capernaum, a Roman officer came and pleaded with him, "Lord, my young servant lies in bed, paralyzed and in terrible pain."*
>
> *Jesus said, "I will come and heal him."*
>
> *But the officer said, "Lord, I am not worthy to have you come into my home. Just say the word from where you are, and my servant will be healed. I know this because I am under the authority of my superior officers, and I have authority over my soldiers. I only need to say, 'Go,' and they go, or 'Come,' and they come. And if I say to my slaves, 'Do this,' they do it."*
>
> *When Jesus heard this, he was amazed. Turning to those who were following him, he said, "I tell you the truth, I haven't seen faith like this in all Israel! And I tell you this, that many Gentiles will come from all over the world—from east and west—and sit down with Abraham, Isaac, and Jacob at the feast in the Kingdom of Heaven.*

> *But many Israelites—those for whom the Kingdom was prepared—will be thrown into outer darkness, where there will be weeping and gnashing of teeth."*
>
> *Then Jesus said to the Roman officer, "Go back home. Because you believed, it has happened." And the young servant was healed that same hour* (Matthew 8:5-13, New Living Translation).

Jesus also responded to the faith of a horribly marginalized Canaanite woman who came pleading for her demon-possessed daughter. Again, he recognizes that she — a foreigner — has *great* faith!

> *Then Jesus left Galilee and went north to the region of Tyre and Sidon. A Gentile woman who lived there came to him, pleading, "Have mercy on me, O Lord, Son of David! For my daughter is possessed by a demon that torments her severely."*
>
> *But Jesus gave her no reply, not even a word. Then his disciples urged him to send her away. "Tell her to go away," they said. "She is bothering us with all her begging."*
>
> *Then Jesus said to the woman, "I was sent only to help God's lost sheep—the people of Israel."*
>
> *But she came and worshiped him, pleading again, "Lord, help me!"*
>
> *Jesus responded, "It isn't right to take food from the children and throw it to the dogs."*
>
> *She replied, "That's true, Lord, but even dogs are allowed to eat the scraps that fall beneath their masters' table."*
>
> *"Dear woman," Jesus said to her, "your faith is great. Your request is granted." And her daughter was instantly healed* (Matthew 15:21-28, New Living Translation).

Jesus did not heal and deliver everyone around him, but he was intent on bringing healing and deliverance to those who sought him out in faith. The sick, the demonized, the hated, the marginalized, the foreigner — Jesus made time for each of them as they showed the Holy Spirit had already planted the seeds of real (even great) faith in their hearts. Whether it was Jesus' prayer relationship with his Heavenly Father, or the indwelling presence of the Holy Spirit with him from the time of his baptism (most likely, it was both), he was able to see past all those who were not yet made ready to those who were "low hanging fruit." These were precious men, women and children from different backgrounds, with different situations (some desperate) and even from different people groups that had been prepared for their own Jesus-encounter. And we also cannot neglect the fact that in nearly every case, the ripple effect we talked about in Chapter 1 impacts multitudes through low hanging fruit encounters.

The Apostles and "Low Hanging Fruit" People

Jesus taught his disciples well. They followed their rabbi's example and were quick and faithful to recognize low hanging fruit as they went through their daily lives. Let's look at five specific examples. I pray that these will be instructive to us so we also may partner with the Holy Spirit, being ever ready to bless those around us with the love, ministry and witness of our Jesus.

Peter, John and the Crippled Beggar

We looked at this encounter before, but let's make it a little more personal. This beggar is a man — a precious soul to God and a child of Abraham. From other sources, we believe he was likely over 30 years of age. We also know he had been crippled from birth. This man had never known ambulatory freedom. He had always been dependent on others for everything: transportation, provision, everything. Every single day he was carried (presumably by friends) to the Beautiful Gate of the Temple to beg for a living. Every day for his whole life — or at least his whole adult life.

> *Peter and John went to the Temple one afternoon to take part in the three o'clock prayer service. As they approached the Temple, a man lame from birth was being carried in. Each day he was put beside the Temple gate, the one called the Beautiful Gate, so he could beg from the people going into the Temple. When he saw Peter and John about to enter, he asked them for some money.*
>
> *Peter and John looked at him intently, and Peter said, "Look at us!" The lame man looked at them eagerly, expecting some money.*

> *But Peter said, "I don't have any silver or gold for you. But I'll give you what I have. In the name of Jesus Christ the Nazarene, get up and walk!"*
>
> *Then Peter took the lame man by the right hand and helped him up. And as he did, the man's feet and ankles were instantly healed and strengthened. He jumped up, stood on his feet, and began to walk! Then, walking, leaping, and praising God, he went into the Temple with them.*
>
> *All the people saw him walking and heard him praising God. When they realized he was the lame beggar they had seen so often at the Beautiful Gate, they were absolutely astounded! They all rushed out in amazement to Solomon's Colonnade, where the man was holding tightly to Peter and John* (Acts 3:1-11, New Living Translation).

Begging was this man's life. According to the passage, he had his regular spot at this particular gate. He was there every single day. Every. Single. Day. But on this particular day, the Holy Spirit was orchestrating a surprise. He had everything in place. He had been tweaking the man's own faith in some way. He had already prepared two lead apostles who seem to take this route on a regular basis. And he had gathered a wider crowd in that space to blow them away with God's goodness and power. The rest is biblical history. And the awe and wonder of it all changed many lives that day.

Philip and the Ethiopian Eunuch

This one has an exciting cross-cultural flavor. This story starts with an angel's prompting — but whether it's one of God's holy messengers or the Holy Spirit, heaven is calling on Philip to pay close attention.

> *As for Philip, an angel of the Lord said to him, "Go south down the desert road that runs from Jerusalem to Gaza." So he started out, and he met the treasurer of Ethiopia, a eunuch of great authority under the Kandake, the queen of Ethiopia. The eunuch had gone to Jerusalem to worship, and he was now returning. Seated in his carriage, he was reading aloud from the book of the prophet Isaiah.*

The Holy Spirit said to Philip, "Go over and walk along beside the carriage."

Philip ran over and heard the man reading from the prophet Isaiah. Philip asked, "Do you understand what you are reading?"

The man replied, "How can I, unless someone instructs me?" And he urged Philip to come up into the carriage and sit with him.

The passage of Scripture he had been reading was this:

> *"He was led like a sheep to the slaughter.*
>
> *And as a lamb is silent before the shearers,*
>
> *he did not open his mouth.*
>
> *He was humiliated and received no justice.*
>
> *Who can speak of his descendants?*
>
> *For his life was taken from the earth."*

The eunuch asked Philip, "Tell me, was the prophet talking about himself or someone else?" So beginning with this same Scripture, Philip told him the Good News about Jesus.

As they rode along, they came to some water, and the eunuch said, "Look! There's some water! Why can't I be baptized?" He ordered the carriage to stop, and they went down into the water, and Philip baptized him.

When they came up out of the water, the Spirit of the Lord snatched Philip away. The eunuch never saw him again but went on his way rejoicing. Meanwhile, Philip found himself farther north at the town of Azotus. He preached the Good News there and in every town along the way until he came to Caesarea (Acts 8:26-40, New Living Translation).

Have you ever felt God's prompting within and what you thought he was saying just didn't make sense? As I read this passage, I've always wondered if that wasn't Philip's experience here. An angel confronts him and tells him to walk down a specific road. It appears that Philip didn't question it — he obeys and he meets up with the treasurer of Ethiopia.

I love this account because it beautifully displays the Holy Spirit's handiwork. Not only is Philip ready and willing to obey the prompts, but do you see how the Spirit has already prepared the eunuch? He has come to Jerusalem to worship — so, his heart is already transformed enough to desire to worship God, likely at or near the Temple. This is particularly interesting because he is a eunuch. The Law (Deuteronomy 23:1) says that eunuch's may not worship in the Temple. And yet, Isaiah later prophesied:

> *"Don't let foreigners who commit themselves to the Lord say,*
> *'The Lord will never let me be part of his people.'*
> *And don't let the eunuchs say,*
> *'I'm a dried-up tree with no children and no future.'*
> *For this is what the Lord says:*
> *I will bless those eunuchs*
> *who keep my Sabbath days holy*
> *and who choose to do what pleases me*
> *and commit their lives to me.*
> *I will give them—within the walls of my house—*
> *a memorial and a name*
> *far greater than sons and daughters could give.*
> *For the name I give them is an everlasting one.*
> *It will never disappear!* (Isaiah 56:3-5, New Living Translation).

The Holy Spirit has orchestrated that Philip and the eunuch would meet in this, God's perfect timing. Further, he had the eunuch reading from the Scroll of Isaiah as Philip neared the chariot. What was he reading? Isaiah 53 — the most blatant description of the work of Jesus, the Messiah, in his loving sacrifice for the redemption of humanity.

> *"He was led like a sheep to the slaughter.*
> *And as a lamb is silent before the shearers,*
> *he did not open his mouth.*
> *He was humiliated and received no justice.*
> *Who can speak of his descendants?*

For his life was taken from the earth" (Acts 8:32-33, quoting from Isaiah 53. Please take some time to read Isaiah's whole chapter. It's only 12 verses).

Philip initiates a conversation based upon what he had just heard the eunuch read and, in that moment, the gospel begins its breakthrough to the people of Ethiopia!

Peter and a Gentile Centurion Named Cornelius

Have you ever argued with God? Did you ever think God may be leading you to do something you did not expect because of the incredible gospel impact it would have? That's what happened to Peter. He was praying and worshipping God on the roof one day (not an unusual place to be in first century Israel, by the way, as people often had living space on their roofs).

> *In Caesarea there lived a Roman army officer named Cornelius, who was a captain of the Italian Regiment. He was a devout, God-fearing man, as was everyone in his household. He gave generously to the poor and prayed regularly to God. One afternoon about three o'clock, he had a vision in which he saw an angel of God coming toward him. "Cornelius!" the angel said.*
>
> *Cornelius stared at him in terror. "What is it, sir?" he asked the angel.*
>
> *And the angel replied, "Your prayers and gifts to the poor have been received by God as an offering! Now send some men to Joppa, and summon a man named Simon Peter. He is staying with Simon, a tanner who lives near the seashore."*
>
> *As soon as the angel was gone, Cornelius called two of his household servants and a devout soldier, one of his personal attendants. He told them what had happened and sent them off to Joppa.*
>
> *The next day as Cornelius's messengers were nearing the town, Peter went up on the flat roof to pray. It was about noon, and he was hungry. But while a meal was being prepared, he fell into a trance. He saw the sky open, and something like a large sheet was*

let down by its four corners. In the sheet were all sorts of animals, reptiles, and birds. Then a voice said to him, "Get up, Peter; kill and eat them."

"No, Lord," Peter declared. "I have never eaten anything that our Jewish laws have declared impure and unclean."

But the voice spoke again: "Do not call something unclean if God has made it clean." The same vision was repeated three times. Then the sheet was suddenly pulled up to heaven.

Peter was very perplexed. What could the vision mean? Just then the men sent by Cornelius found Simon's house. Standing outside the gate, they asked if a man named Simon Peter was staying there.

Meanwhile, as Peter was puzzling over the vision, the Holy Spirit said to him, "Three men have come looking for you. Get up, go downstairs, and go with them without hesitation. Don't worry, for I have sent them."

So Peter went down and said, "I'm the man you are looking for. Why have you come?"

There is so much in this story! The Holy Spirit is simultaneously working on the heart of a Roman Centurion to grow his God-fearing devotion into full faith in Jesus, and is dealing with one of the lead apostles of Jesus about his religious prejudices. The Spirit had been working on Cornelius' whole household to prepare them for the coming encounter. God had to show Peter that he intends to make good on the prophecies about reaching the Gentiles and that Peter needs to get with the program. God sends Cornelius an angel, and humorously, he sends Peter a vision of unclean foods. He orchestrates a meeting, bringing the Gentile servants to Peter so Peter can follow them back to Joppa and Cornelius.

If we were to keep reading in Acts 10, we would see that the Spirit-led encounter would not only see many Gentiles saved that day, but filled with the Holy Spirit. Paul may have been the Apostle to the Gentiles, but it was Peter who was first used by the Holy Spirit to break through the Gentile barrier. What we've called the "ripple effect" on this one was huge.

Paul, Silas and Lydia the Seller of Purple

The story of Lydia's conversion is another beautiful story of low hanging fruit.

> *We boarded a boat at Troas and sailed straight across to the island of Samothrace, and the next day we landed at Neapolis. From there we reached Philippi, a major city of that district of Macedonia and a Roman colony. And we stayed there several days.*
>
> *On the Sabbath we went a little way outside the city to a riverbank, where we thought people would be meeting for prayer, and we sat down to speak with some women who had gathered there. One of them was Lydia from Thyatira, a merchant of expensive purple cloth, who worshiped God. As she listened to us, the Lord opened her heart, and she accepted what Paul was saying. She and her household were baptized, and she asked us to be her guests. "If you agree that I am a true believer in the Lord," she said, "come and stay at my home." And she urged us until we agreed* (Acts 16:11-15, New Living Translation).

Paul and Silas were following their regular weekly routine and were looking for a place to celebrate the Sabbath. They gathered where they expected people to be meeting for prayer. All in a normal day's activity, they just struck up a Sabbath conversation with some women there (while that may have been a little unusual for the old Paul, he was no longer stuck in his Pharisaical trappings). One of these ladies was Lydia. Lydia was a wealthy business woman from Thytira. But she had also been a loving target of the Holy Spirit. By the time she meets Paul and Silas, she is already a worshipper of God.

Staying true to form, Paul turns the conversation in a spiritual direction. Notice that the scripture says "the Lord opened her heart and she accepted what Paul was saying" (Acts 16:14). The Holy Spirit does it again — and this time he continues the work through Lydia and the Philippian church is planted in her home (Acts 16:40)!

New Testament Examples

Paul, Silas and a Philippian Jailer

Beautifully linked to the story of Lydia is the story of a Philippian jailer who was given the task of guarding Paul and Silas after their arrest for delivering a girl from a future-telling demon, keeping her in lucrative bondage to her masters. Once the evil spirit was cast out, her owners saw their money source dry up and they caused a ruckus.

Did you know that there is even low hanging fruit in jail? It's true. And here Paul and Silas are imprisoned and awaiting their trial. At midnight, they are praying and singing hymns to God.

> *Around midnight Paul and Silas were praying and singing hymns to God, and the other prisoners were listening. Suddenly, there was a massive earthquake, and the prison was shaken to its foundations. All the doors immediately flew open, and the chains of every prisoner fell off! The jailer woke up to see the prison doors wide open. He assumed the prisoners had escaped, so he drew his sword to kill himself. But Paul shouted to him, "Stop! Don't kill yourself! We are all here!"*
>
> *The jailer called for lights and ran to the dungeon and fell down trembling before Paul and Silas. Then he brought them out and asked, "Sirs, what must I do to be saved?"*
>
> *They replied, "Believe in the Lord Jesus and you will be saved, along with everyone in your household." And they shared the word of the Lord with him and with all who lived in his household. Even at that hour of the night, the jailer cared for them and washed their wounds. Then he and everyone in his household were immediately baptized. He brought them into his house and set a meal before them, and he and his entire household rejoiced because they all believed in God* (Acts 16:25-34, New Living Translation).

Maintaining their composure, their witness and remaining observant even in jail gave Paul and Silas their next low hanging fruit opportunity. Their witness covered all those who were imprisoned with them (Acts 16:25). The Holy Spirit brought about an earthquake to set the stage for his next encounter. Shackles fell off and jail doors were opened, but surprisingly nobody left (Acts 16:28). In the Roman Empire, jailers guarded their prisoners under penalty of their own death if there was a breach. But there wasn't. Did you catch the question the jailer asked upon seeing that his life was safe because none had escaped? The Holy Spirit used the jailer's own dire circumstances to finish the job. And that night, his entire household was saved and *immediately* baptized (Acts 16:33).

In each of these examples — both those with Jesus and those with his apostles — the people were prepared by the Holy Spirit for their encounter. The Spirit prepares his servants. The Spirit prepares the hearts of those he plans to reach. And then the Spirit orchestrates the circumstances so that each low hanging fruit encounter works exactly as planned. He prepares everything so that lost souls will experience the love, grace, ministry and witness of God's people. And he still does this today.

PART TWO

Building Redemptive Relationships

CHAPTER 3
Building Redemptive Relationships (Part 1)

One day as Jesus was walking along the shore of the Sea of Galilee, he saw two brothers—Simon, also called Peter, and Andrew—throwing a net into the water, for they fished for a living. Jesus called out to them, "Come, follow me, and I will show you how to fish for people!" And they left their nets at once and followed him
(Matthew 4:18-20, New Living Translation).

We now come to the foundation of reaching low hanging fruit people: building redemptive relationships. This is so critical to the success of reaching our low hanging fruit friends and coworkers that I have purposefully spread this material over two chapters to make it more manageable. Don't rush this portion of your reading. Let the Holy Spirit speak to you about the relationships you might already have where he has been working.

Earlier in this book we talked about how Philip's encounter with the Ethiopian eunuch was a great example of low hanging fruit. There clearly are times when the Holy Spirit will call upon us to meet with someone we do not know but whom he has prepared for that moment. I've had those encounters myself. But we need to understand that these are the exception, not the rule. In most cases, low hanging fruit people will be people with whom you have a relationship — either an existing one or a new one that you will need to develop. Immediate fruit like the salvation and baptism of the eunuch do indeed happen, but much more of your work will be in the lives of people with whom you are on the journey of life.

To help us better understand this longer-term, life-on-life ministry principle, we will now turn to Jesus' relationship with Peter. Peter had learned the Torah like all young Jewish boys. And as he got a little older, he was likely trained in the other books — the Writings and the Prophets — by both his father and a local rabbi. But at that critical juncture when all Jewish boys become teens and their life's path is being determined, Peter was not selected by his rabbi for further training. He had learned what all Jewish men would learn, so they could live and worship rightly, but he was not considered promising enough to become a rabbi himself. And so, like other young men passed over by the rabbis, Peter (as well as his brother Andrew) joined the family business and became a fisherman. We pick up Peter's story with Jesus on the rocky shore of the Sea of Galilee (the modern Lake Kinneret). Jesus built a redemptive relationship with Peter. And while we will focus on Peter in this chapter, please know that what we will describe is true in every low hanging fruit relationship.

The Invitation

Redemptive relationships are intentional. They have a goal of creating an ongoing life-on-life environment where we can invest in someone, leading them toward Christian maturity. Every redemptive relationship begins with an invitation of some kind. Even when we already have an existing relationship with someone — a friend, colleague, or even family member — there comes a point where we intentionally invite them deeper. This is what Jesus did with each of his disciples, including a young man named Peter.

> *One day as Jesus was preaching on the shore of the Sea of Galilee, great crowds pressed in on him to listen to the word of God. He noticed two empty boats at the water's edge, for the fishermen had left them and were washing their nets. Stepping into one of the boats, Jesus asked Simon, its owner, to push it out into the water. So he sat in the boat and taught the crowds from there.*

> *When he had finished speaking, he said to Simon, "Now go out where it is deeper, and let down your nets to catch some fish."*
>
> *"Master," Simon replied, "we worked hard all last night and didn't catch a thing. But if you say so, I'll let the nets down again." And this time their nets were so full of fish they began to tear! A shout for help brought their partners in the other boat, and soon both boats were filled with fish and on the verge of sinking.*
>
> *When Simon Peter realized what had happened, he fell to his knees before Jesus and said, "Oh, Lord, please leave me—I'm such a sinful man." For he was awestruck by the number of fish they had caught, as were the others with him. his partners, James and John, the sons of Zebedee, were also amazed.*
>
> *Jesus replied to Simon, "Don't be afraid! From now on you'll be fishing for people!" And as soon as they landed, they left everything and followed Jesus* (Luke 5:1-11, New Living Translation).

We prayerfully invite people into a deeper relationship. These are usually folks in whom we are already seeing low hanging fruit evidence. We invite them to grow with us spiritually — to learn the scriptures together, to pray together, to serve together, to worship together. Not everyone will accept such an invitation. That is to be expected. Rejection even happened to Jesus (see John 6:60-69 and Matthew 19:16-22). But some will accept the offer, and this is likely an indication of low hanging fruit. Typically, each of us only has a few of these relationships at any given time.

The Basics of Kingdom Culture

Once someone accepts our invitation, we begin helping them understand and grow in Jesus' kingdom culture. The culture of this world has been made upside down and backward by the enemy of our souls. The culture of Jesus' kingdom is rightside up — but that seems strange to those who are still of the world. Jesus introduces Peter (and his other disciples) to this intended culture in the Beatitudes.

> *One day as he saw the crowds gathering, Jesus went up on the mountainside and sat down. His disciples gathered around him, and he began to teach them.*

> *"God blesses those who are poor and realize their need for him, for the Kingdom of Heaven is theirs.*
>
> *God blesses those who mourn, for they will be comforted.*
>
> *God blesses those who are humble,*
>
> *for they will inherit the whole earth.*
>
> *God blesses those who hunger and thirst for justice,*
>
> *for they will be satisfied.*
>
> *God blesses those who are merciful,*
>
> *for they will be shown mercy.*
>
> *God blesses those whose hearts are pure,*
>
> *for they will see God.*
>
> *God blesses those who work for peace,*
>
> *for they will be called the children of God.*
>
> *God blesses those who are persecuted for doing right,*
>
> *for the Kingdom of Heaven is theirs.*
>
> "God blesses you when people mock you and persecute you and lie about you and say all sorts of evil things against you because you are my followers. Be happy about it! Be very glad! For a great reward awaits you in heaven. And remember, the ancient prophets were persecuted in the same way (Matthew 5:1-12, New Living Translation).

Jesus' culture may first seem odd to low hanging fruit people, but they will begin to see its value. They will learn that there is true greatness in being a servant. They will learn that real life is found in sacrifice. They will learn that this world has it all wrong. This was the new learning journey Peter was on, but it didn't stop there.

After the Beatitudes, Jesus continues his lesson by describing kingdom life and behavior in what we call The Sermon on the Mount (Matthew 5:13-7:29). He bases his discourse on a fuller rabbinical understanding of The Ten Commandments. Peter and the disciples were in for quite a ride — as are we! Jesus sets the standard for us on these redemptive relationships. We are not just to convey sound biblical *information*, but to partner with the Holy Spirit to foster kingdom *transformation*. With our invitation comes the challenge of living the kingdom culture out. With our instruction comes accountability.

The Lesson on Prayer

Right in the midst of the Sermon on the Mount, Jesus teaches Peter and the rest how to correctly approach the Father in prayer. We will go into more detail on praying with low hanging fruit people in chapter 5, but one of the most important things we can do in these redemptive relationships is teach our own "disciples" how to pray. We have Jesus' lesson on prayer to his own followers recorded in Matthew 6:5-15 and also in Luke 11:1-13. This lesson is not just about the mechanics of prayer, but is intended to teach us how to live out the prayer *relationship* we are to have with our heavenly Father.

The Demonstration of Kingdom Authority

There are two kingdoms described in the New Testament: the kingdom of darkness (the rule and reign of Satan), and the kingdom of light (the rule and reign of Jesus). Jesus takes on the kingdom of darkness directly in both his teaching and his ministry. And he teaches his disciples to do the same.

> *When the seventy-two disciples returned, they joyfully reported to him, "Lord, even the demons obey us when we use your name!"*
>
> *"Yes," he told them, "I saw Satan fall from heaven like lightning! Look, I have given you authority over all the power of the enemy, and you can walk among snakes and scorpions and crush them. Nothing will injure you. But don't rejoice because evil spirits obey you; rejoice because your names are registered in heaven"* (Luke 10:17-20, New Living Translation).

The Apostle Paul understands his own calling as a mission to move people from the kingdom of darkness to the kingdom of light. Reporting to King Agrippa about his encounter with the risen Christ on the road to Damascus, Paul quotes Jesus as saying,

> *Yes, I am sending you to the Gentiles to open their eyes, so they may turn from darkness to light and from the power of Satan to God. Then they will receive forgiveness for their sins and be given a place among God's people, who are set apart by faith in me'* (Acts 26:17-18, New Living Translation).

And the Apostle Peter informs the whole church that we have all been called out of one kingdom and into another. It's part of the good news we now proclaim.

> *But you are not like that, for you are a chosen people. You are royal priests, a holy nation, God's very own possession. As a result, you can show others the goodness of God, for he called you out of the darkness into his wonderful light* (1 Peter 2:9, New Living Translation).

Destroying Satan's work and overtaking his kingdom, Jesus leads Peter and the other disciples through a series of hands-on lessons where he demonstrates the absolute authority of his kingdom. Each demonstration is a kingdom to kingdom confrontation. For example, in Matthew 8:1-17 we see:

- Jesus heals a man with leprosy by *touching him* (vv. 1-4)
- Jesus heals the servant of a Roman Centurion with only a command (vv. 5-13)
- Jesus heals many and also delivers many from demons (vv. 14-17)

Here is the point: we have the same kingdom authority that Jesus has, because he gave it to us (see Chapter 1). Jesus is 100% God *and* 100% human. But it's important to note that, with the exception of the transfiguration (Luke 9:28-36) and his post resurrection appearances, Jesus lived and did ministry fully as a human being. In order to fulfill his mission to perfectly substitute for us in his sacrificial death, he had to live a perfect human life (Philippians 2:5-8; Hebrews 4:15). He taught with authority, not because he was God, but because he was a human being filled with the Holy Spirit — the Spirit of truth (John 14:17). He healed and delivered people, not because he was God, but because he was a human being filled with the Holy Spirit — the Spirit of Healing (1 Corinthians 12:9). He raised the dead, not because he was God, but because he was a human being filled with the Holy Spirit — the same Spirit that raised Jesus from the dead (Romans 8:11)! And we have the same Holy Spirit!

We have been deputized in the Great Commission (Matthew 28:18-20). We have been "called" as ambassadors of Jesus Christ — the King of all kings (2 Corinthians 5:20). We have the same Holy Spirit (Acts 1:8). Therefore, we can do the same — and even greater — works as Jesus (John 14:12)! It's our turn to confront the kingdom of darkness. And we need to show our low hanging fruit friends this authority as well — because one day we hope they are wielding it with us side by side.

The First Test

There will be many tests in these redemptive relationships. Remember, our relationship with low hanging fruit people is not to increase their knowledge alone, but to increase their faithful obedience to Jesus. It appears that Peter's first real test of faith was a great storm that arose as the disciples were crossing the Sea of Galilee.

> *Then Jesus got into the boat and started across the lake with his disciples. Suddenly, a fierce storm struck the lake, with waves breaking into the boat. But Jesus was sleeping. The disciples went and woke him up, shouting, "Lord, save us! We're going to drown!"*
>
> *Jesus responded, "Why are you afraid? You have so little faith!" Then he got up and rebuked the wind and waves, and suddenly there was a great calm.*
>
> *The disciples were amazed. "Who is this man?" they asked. "Even the winds and waves obey him!"* (Matthew 8:23-27, New Living Translation).

Peter, Andrew, James and John were all seasoned fishermen. They had their own boats and were quite used to sailing in and across the Sea of

Galilee. They basically grew up on it. So when a storm causes seasoned fishermen to fear, it must have been a big one! Jesus slept — the fishermen panicked. It was a test.

Anyone who has pursued a deeper faith walk with Jesus also knows this kind of testing. We've all had our "storms" that we've had to endure. The Holy Spirit uses familiar things to test the mettle of our faith. As a pastor I can recount many tests that were built on various areas of ministry. A friend who is a Christian psychologist tells of a time when he was in crisis and was forced to walk through the same advice he had given countless others. The fishermen were tested in their own boats on a familiar part of the Sea.

Tests like this are what ultimately move low-hanging fruit people into deeper faith, but they can be hard to watch. The key is that our low-hanging fruit friends don't traverse them alone. Jesus was in the boat with Peter and his colleagues. Your low hanging fruit friends have you. They will look to you for comfort and guidance. They will beg for your prayers. They will want to hear of your experience in similar circumstances. And they might need help — at least at first — seeing Jesus in the midst of their test. Help them.

The Challenge to Practice.

Jesus also challenges Peter (and the other disciples) to actually put what they are learning into practice. There are a couple of scenarios in scripture that are helpful for us on this point. The first unfolds as Jesus is traveling around teaching and shows his disciples the dire needs of the people.

> *Jesus traveled through all the towns and villages of that area, teaching in the synagogues and announcing the Good News about the Kingdom. And he healed every kind of disease and illness. When he saw the crowds, he had compassion on them because they were confused and helpless, like sheep without a shepherd. He said to his disciples, "The harvest is great, but the workers are few. So pray to the Lord who is in charge of the harvest; ask him to send more workers into his fields"* (Matthew 9:35-38, New Living Translation).

Immediately following this statement, Jesus sends out the twelve to actually *do* what he has been demonstrating to them. Recall Jesus' purpose statement from Luke 4 and Isaiah 61:

> *"The Spirit of the Lord is upon me,*
> *for he has anointed me to bring Good News to the poor.*
> *He has sent me to proclaim that captives will be released,*
> *that the blind will see, that the oppressed will be set free,*
> *and that the time of the Lord's favor has come"*
> (Luke 4:18-19, New Living Translation).

Jesus shows Peter and the rest the plight of the people he came to save. He helps them all be moved with compassion. He announces that the laborers needed to reach this incredible harvest are too few. And then Jesus sends them out to continue the work that he, himself has been doing. They get to practice what they've learned.

The second scenario comes with a miraculous meal.

> *That evening the disciples came to him and said, "This is a remote place, and it's already getting late. Send the crowds away so they can go to the villages and buy food for themselves."*
>
> *But Jesus said, "That isn't necessary—you feed them."*
>
> *"But we have only five loaves of bread and two fish!" they answered.*
>
> *"Bring them here," he said. Then he told the people to sit down on the grass. Jesus took the five loaves and two fish, looked up toward heaven, and blessed them. Then, breaking the loaves into pieces, he gave the bread to the disciples, who distributed it to the people. They all ate as much as they wanted, and afterward, the disciples picked up twelve baskets of leftovers. About 5,000 men were fed that day, in addition to all the women and children! (Matthew 14:15-21, New Living Translation)*

When one counts all who were present for this miracle, some estimate it may have been as many as 15,000 to 18,000 people. The disciples see the crowd that has followed their rabbi and know it's going to be impossible for them all to get food. So they do the "sensible" thing and suggest to Jesus that they all be sent away. But Jesus has a different idea. Did you catch his response?

*But Jesus said, "That isn't necessary—**you feed them**"* (Matthew 14:16, New Living Translation, **emphasis mine**).

They've seen him work miracles, but they still aren't on the same page. What begins as a test of their faith leads to an opportunity to, once again, practice. The challenge is a big one — but Jesus delivers. He multiplies five loaves of bread and two fish and feeds 18,000 people to their fill! But Jesus' work was only to bless the food — it was Peter and the crew that had to distribute it to all those people.

Again, Peter is not to become an academic; he is to be a practitioner. It's like developing a muscle — it takes *doing* not just *knowing.* Jesus challenges his protege so he learns how to actually do what his rabbi is demonstrating. There will be disbelief. There will be mistakes. There will be outright failure. But each challenge is designed to take Peter steadily deeper into his faith walk with Jesus.

We also must challenge our low hanging fruit friends so they can grow in a similar fashion. We join them in the laboratory of application when it comes to prayer and intercession, worship, rest and retreat, service, witness and more. We point them to opportunities where they can put what they are learning into practice. The result will nearly always be noticeable growth in their walk with Jesus.

The Family

Jesus did something with Peter, James and John — and likely with the other disciples — that may have been unusual for a first century rabbi. He made them his family. They weren't just his students or servants in a synagogue, they were family-level friends.

> *This is my commandment: Love each other in the same way I have loved you. There is no greater love than to lay down one's life for one's friends. You are my friends if you do what I command. I no longer call you slaves, because a master doesn't confide in his*

slaves. Now you are my friends, since I have told you everything the Father told me. You didn't choose me. I chose you. I appointed you to go and produce lasting fruit, so that the Father will give you whatever you ask for, using my name. This is my command: Love each other (John 15:12-17, New Living Translation).

And Jesus wasn't shy about his intentions. In fact, he was quite public about the difference between his blood relatives who did not yet believe in him, and those who had become faithful followers doing the will of his Father.

As Jesus was speaking to the crowd, his mother and brothers stood outside, asking to speak to him. Someone told Jesus, "Your mother and your brothers are standing outside, and they want to speak to you."

Jesus asked, "Who is my mother? Who are my brothers?" then he pointed to his disciples and said, "Look, these are my mother and brothers. Anyone who does the will of my Father in heaven is my brother and sister and mother!" (Matthew 12:46-50, New Living Translation).

Finally, the level of love and trust that grew between Jesus and his disciples — especially the inner core of Peter, James and John — was immense. So much so that Jesus turned the care of his mother over to John ("the disciple whom Jesus loved") even though he had siblings by Mary at the time of his death.

Standing near the cross were Jesus' mother, and his mother's sister, Mary (the wife of Clopas), and Mary Magdalene. When Jesus saw his mother standing there beside the disciple he loved, he said to her, "Dear woman, here is your son." And he said to this disciple, "Here is your mother." And from then on this disciple took her into his home (John 19:25-27, New Living Translation).

In our world today, fewer and fewer people have really good, healthy family and friend relationships. Loneliness is off the charts in our society even though social media and technology makes us more connected than ever. One of the greatest tools the Father has given us for his kingdom purposes is our love (John 13:34-35). It won't be possible or appropriate for every person, but at least some of the low hanging fruit relationships we develop should ultimately go deep. This requires trust — which must be built over time. This requires transparency and vulnerability in the relationship. But for some, such a familial bond will be life-changing. Again, Jesus had a deep and daily relationship with all twelve of his disciples, but it's clear that there was a still deeper level that he offered to his inner three.

CHAPTER 4
Building Redemptive Relationships (Part 2)

The next day Jesus decided to go to Galilee. He found Philip and said to him, "Come, follow me." Philip was from Bethsaida, Andrew and Peter's hometown.

Philip went to look for Nathanael and told him, "We have found the very person Moses and the prophets wrote about! His name is Jesus, the son of Joseph from Nazareth."

"Nazareth!" exclaimed Nathanael. "Can anything good come from Nazareth?"

"Come and see for yourself," Philip replied.

As they approached, Jesus said, "Now here is a genuine son of Israel—a man of complete integrity."

"How do you know about me?" Nathanael asked.

Jesus replied, "I could see you under the fig tree before Philip found you."

Then Nathanael exclaimed, "Rabbi, you are the Son of God—the King of Israel!"

Jesus asked him, "Do you believe this just because I told you I had seen you under the fig tree? You will see greater things than this."

Then he said, "I tell you the truth, you will all see heaven open and the angels of God going up and down on the Son of Man, the one who is the stairway between heaven and earth" (John 1:43-51, New Living Translation).

We now pick up where we left off in the last chapter on building redemptive relationships. When a low hanging fruit person's faith really begins to grow, exciting things happen!

Miracle-working Faith

Growing the faith of low hanging fruit people is always the ultimate goal of these relationships. We must continuously beckon them to trust Jesus more fully, obey him more consistently, and to take literal steps of faith in order to keep growing. For Peter, my favorite example of this has always been the day he stepped out of the boat where there was no land in sight.

Immediately after this, Jesus insisted that his disciples get back into the boat and cross to the other side of the lake, while he sent the people home. After sending them home, he went up into the hills by himself to pray. Night fell while he was there alone.

Meanwhile, the disciples were in trouble far away from land, for a strong wind had risen, and they were fighting heavy waves. About three o'clock in the morning Jesus came toward them, walking on the water. When the disciples saw him walking on the water, they were terrified. In their fear, they cried out, "It's a ghost!"

But Jesus spoke to them at once. "Don't be afraid," he said. "Take courage. I am here!"

Then Peter called to him, "Lord, if it's really you, tell me to come to you, walking on the water."

"Yes, come," Jesus said.

So Peter went over the side of the boat and walked on the water toward Jesus. But when he saw the strong wind and the waves, he was terrified and began to sink. "Save me, Lord!" he shouted.

Jesus immediately reached out and grabbed him. "You have so little faith," Jesus said. "Why did you doubt me?"

When they climbed back into the boat, the wind stopped. Then the disciples worshiped him. "You really are the Son of God!" they exclaimed (Matthew 12:22-33, New Living Translation).

People always focus on Peter's faithless plunge beneath the surface. But for me, it's this phrase that stops me in awe:

So Peter went over the side of the boat and walked on the water toward Jesus (Matthew 14:29b, New Living Translation).

There are great sermons preached about how Peter was distracted by the storm. But before he took his eyes off of Jesus, he actually walked on the water! We're not told how far — but it was far enough for Matthew to record that he did it! Peter had enough faith (momentary as it was) to actually defy the laws of physics and do the miraculous at the call of Jesus. This is hugely instructional for us as well.

We keep coming back to more spectacular things: healings, deliverance, walking on water. But the reasons are important. Followers of Christ represent the inbreaking of a new kingdom — a new dominion — that sets everything right (1 Peter 2:9-10). We take on the sin, corruption and damage Satan has wreaked on both people and the rest of creation, and we show that God's way is right, is best, and has the ability to fully overcome every obstacle in its way.

Many Christians today largely practice a Faith without miracles. It's intellectual. It's theological. It's academic. But it appears powerless. If the real kingdom of Jesus is breaking forth into our corrupt, sinful world, there will be demonstrations of its authority and power to go along with the truth we proclaim. Jesus' purpose as first declared by Isaiah is still true (Luke 4:18-19). We bring the Good News, yes. But it is accompanied by captives (literal captives, but also those in bondage to drugs, alcohol, gambling, trafficking and more) being set free! The blind (spiritually blind, yes, but also literal blindness) being healed so they can see! Just as with Jesus' own earthly ministry, the kingdom advancement under us should see the lame to walk, the deaf to hear, lepers cleansed, and even the dead raised. Remember, Jesus told us:

> *"I tell you the truth, anyone who believes in me will do the same works I have done, and even greater works, because I am going to be with the Father. You can ask for anything in my name, and I will do it, so that the Son can bring glory to the Father. Yes, ask me for anything in my name, and I will do it!* (John 14:12-14, New Living Translation).

As we walk with our low hanging fruit friends, *we* need to engage the battle. If we strive to keep everything consistent with the Word of God, then we must strive to see this world with the compassion of Christ and use our God-given ambassadorial authority to intervene (Matthew 9:36; 14:14; Mark 1:41; Luke 7:13). And as we step out of the comfort of our own "boats," like Peter we just might do the miraculous — even if we sink a few times in the beginning. As you step out — grab the hand of a low hanging fruit person and take them with you.

The Epiphany

This is the part of this chapter I could not wait to write! The epiphany. The "a-hah." You might know the story. Jesus is walking along with his disciples in the area of Caesarea Philippi. There were many "Caesareas" in the first century. It was a way for a town or region to butter up Caesar. Most were large cities with great things to offer. But very little is even known about Caesarea Philippi. And yet, it goes down in history as the turning point of Jesus' earthly ministry!

> *When Jesus came to the region of Caesarea Philippi, he asked his disciples, "Who do people say that the Son of Man is?"*
>
> *"Well," they replied, "some say John the Baptist, some say Elijah, and others say Jeremiah or one of the other prophets."*
>
> *Then he asked them, "But who do you say I am?"*
>
> *Simon Peter answered, "You are the Messiah, the Son of the living God."*
>
> *Jesus replied, "You are blessed, Simon son of John, because my Father in heaven has revealed this to you. You did not learn this from any human being. Now I say to you that you are Peter (which means 'rock'), and upon this rock I will build my church, and all*

the powers of hell will not conquer it. And I will give you the keys of the Kingdom of Heaven. Whatever you forbid on earth will be forbidden in heaven, and whatever you permit on earth will be permitted in heaven."

Then he sternly warned the disciples not to tell anyone that he was the Messiah (Matthew 16:13-20, New Living Translation).

Peter has an epiphany directly from our Heavenly Father. Up to this point, there were likely many who were wondering if Jesus was the foretold Messiah, but he had not spoken of it directly. Peter's revelation is huge. It means that Jesus' teaching, discipling, ministry and miracles are speaking loudly about his identity. He is indeed the Christ. And the rest of Jesus' earthly ministry flows under that growing knowledge.

When it comes to low hanging fruit people, you will likely see exciting little glimpses of faith as you walk with them in life. They will learn the Bible and bits and pieces will start making sense to them. They will ask deeper and deeper spiritual questions. You'll notice them catching their own words and behavior against the standard of Jesus' kingdom culture. They will grow in their prayer life. They may even rise to the challenge when their fledgling faith is being tested. But at some point, there is an epiphany. And it's glorious!

It's not appropriate for me to tell these kinds of stories about my own disciples (they need to tell their own stories), but I can tell you there is nothing like the moment when Jesus' Messianic lordship breaks through to a low hanging fruit person. If you are blessed to be with them when it happens, it will overwhelm you. But if you have been walking with them for a season, you will likely still be the first person they call when they "get it" that Jesus really is their Everything: their Savior, their Lord, their Friend.

Once your low hanging fruit friend surrenders to Jesus, your relationship with them changes. It's a beautiful thing. You begin to move from a "mentor-protege" relationship to more like partners. The iron-sharpening-iron idea takes on real flesh (Proverbs 27:17).

The Transfiguration

It makes sense that this incredible event would take place *after* Peter's epiphany. Jesus was still Peter's rabbi, but now Peter was beginning to understand things in a new way. It's somewhere in this timeframe that Jesus tells his disciples that he now considers them friends, not just students (John 15:15). Jesus now shows his inner circle — Peter, James and John — who he *really* is.

> *Six days later Jesus took Peter and the two brothers, James and John, and led them up a high mountain to be alone. As the men watched, Jesus' appearance was transformed so that his face shone like the sun, and his clothes became as white as light. Suddenly, Moses and Elijah appeared and began talking with Jesus.*
>
> *Peter exclaimed, "Lord, it's wonderful for us to be here! If you want, I'll make three shelters as memorials—one for you, one for Moses, and one for Elijah."*
>
> *But even as he spoke, a bright cloud overshadowed them, and a voice from the cloud said, "This is my dearly loved Son, who brings me great joy. Listen to him." The disciples were terrified and fell face down on the ground.*
>
> *Then Jesus came over and touched them. "Get up," he said. "Don't be afraid." And when they looked up, Moses and Elijah were gone, and they saw only Jesus.*
>
> *As they went back down the mountain, Jesus commanded them, "Don't tell anyone what you have seen until the Son of Man has been raised from the dead"* (Matthew 17:1-9, New Living Translation).

Jesus let Peter see behind the curtain. Jesus shows Peter his true identity — and the glory that goes with it. Think about this: Peter, James and John were the only ones in that current timeframe who got to see the physical Shekinah glory of God as a blinding cloud overtaking them. This is the Presence of God that rested on and filled the tabernacle (Exodus 40:31). This is the Presence of the Heavenly Father that met with and led the Israelites in the desert (Exodus 16:10; Numbers 9:15-23). This is the Presence of God that filled the Temple (1 Kings 8:10-11; Isaiah 6:1-4). But it had been gone for a very long time (Ezekiel 10 & 11). Jesus' followers will see this cloud again when Jesus is taken from them up into heaven (Acts 1:6-11).

Jesus was "transfigured" before them, displaying all his glory, majesty and beauty — accompanied by Moses and Elijah, and the Shekinah glory again — if only for a few moments. Jesus shows his inner core of three men who he really is.

There comes a point in your relationship with your low hanging fruit friends that you see the transformation in them and you've grown to trust them enough that you can let your guard down. They get to see the real you. You and I don't have God's glory — in fact, we still have "stuff" we're trying to crucify. But there is something powerful that happens when your own disciples know they are seeing the real you. This is where "iron sharpening" begins. Your relationship grows to a new level where you invite *them* to speak into your life to help you grow as well.

The Call to Servanthood

Jesus' final lesson with his disciples is an important one. And true to form, Peter doesn't understand it at first.

> *Before the Passover celebration, Jesus knew that his hour had come to leave this world and return to his Father. He had loved his disciples during his ministry on earth, and now he loved them to the very end. It was time for supper, and the devil had already prompted Judas, son of Simon Iscariot, to betray Jesus. Jesus knew that the Father had given him authority over everything and that he had come from God and would return to God. So he got up from the table, took off his robe, wrapped a towel around his waist, and poured water into a basin. Then he began to wash the disciples' feet, drying them with the towel he had around him.*
>
> *When Jesus came to Simon Peter, Peter said to him, "Lord, are you going to wash my feet?"*
>
> *Jesus replied, "You don't understand now what I am doing, but someday you will."*
>
> *"No," Peter protested, "you will never ever wash my feet!"*

Jesus replied, "Unless I wash you, you won't belong to me."

Simon Peter exclaimed, "Then wash my hands and head as well, Lord, not just my feet!"

Jesus replied, "A person who has bathed all over does not need to wash, except for the feet, to be entirely clean. And you disciples are clean, but not all of you." For Jesus knew who would betray him. That is what he meant when he said, "Not all of you are clean."

After washing their feet, he put on his robe again and sat down and asked, "Do you understand what I was doing? You call me 'Teacher' and 'Lord,' and you are right, because that's what I am. And since I, your Lord and Teacher, have washed your feet, you ought to wash each other's feet. I have given you an example to follow. Do as I have done to you. I tell you the truth, slaves are not greater than their master. Nor is the messenger more important than the one who sends the message. Now that you know these things, God will bless you for doing them (John 13:1-17, New Living Translation).

Pride and self-aggrandizement are enemies to Jesus' kingdom culture. Jesus had a particular problem with religious leaders and rabbis who displayed these traits. His lesson then, and his lesson now is that true greatness is found in service (see Matthew 23:1-12). Jesus demonstrates this critical truth by wrapping a towel around his own waist and washing dirty feet — which was servant's work. Peter reacts to this living illustration of Jesus' compassion and service because he is still caught up in a person's position.

I will never forget a special dinner that happened during the first month of my first senior pastorate. The meal was finished and the people were leaving. I grabbed a small bucket of sanitizing solution and a cloth and began wiping down the tables and chairs before we put them back in storage. One of my deacons tapped me on the back and actually scolded me, "Preacher, that's not your job. We've got this. You go home." I just smiled and told him that all kinds of service was indeed my job because I had to lead by example just like Jesus did. And then I reminded him of

Peter's reaction to Jesus washing his disciples' feet. He talked about that night for years. He'd tell people, "I've never seen a pastor do manual labor before!" (That, of course, is another issue.)

When it comes to service, we must lead by example. We do not tell our low hanging fruit disciples how to do it (although instruction is always appropriate), we *show* them. We serve *together*. We take them along when we'll be serving. And if they have a particular giftedness, we make time to go with them and take part in the learning of their specialization for the kingdom. The key is that teaching, here, is much more than telling. It's partnership.

The Garden Prayer

As the depth of your relational investment into your low hanging fruit friend grows, you've shown them who you really are in Christ and they are aware of the areas where you are still growing, and you've served with them in ministry, most will now have become deeply trusted comrades. This is where they really begin ministering back to you. As Jesus neared the moments of his trial and sacrifice, he went to the Garden of Gethsemane to pray — fervently — before his Heavenly Father.

> *Then Jesus went with them to the olive grove called Gethsemane, and he said, "Sit here while I go over there to pray." He took Peter and Zebedee's two sons, James and John, and he became anguished and distressed. He told them, "My soul is crushed with grief to the point of death. Stay here and keep watch with me."*
>
> *He went on a little farther and bowed with his face to the ground, praying, "My Father! If it is possible, let this cup of suffering be taken away from me. Yet I want your will to be done, not mine."*
>
> *Then he returned to the disciples and found them asleep. He said to Peter, "Couldn't you watch with me even one hour? Keep watch and pray, so that you will not give in to temptation. For the spirit is willing, but the body is weak!"*
>
> *Then Jesus left them a second time and prayed, "My Father! If this cup cannot be taken away unless I drink it, your will be done." When he returned to them again, he found them sleeping, for they couldn't keep their eyes open.*

So he went to pray a third time, saying the same things again. Then he came to the disciples and said, "Go ahead and sleep. Have your rest. But look—the time has come. The Son of Man is betrayed into the hands of sinners. Up, let's be going. Look, my betrayer is here!" (Matthew 26:36-46, New Living Translation)

Jesus is in agony. He was suffering in prayer. His burden was overwhelming. And knowing how he would endure this night's prayer, he invited his three inner-core disciples to accompany him. Peter was with Jesus — not far away — as his friend and rabbi suffered. But even as Jesus suffered and his betrayer was on the move with soldiers for Jesus' arrest, Peter and the others could not stay awake. I expect they had good intentions, but their service back to Jesus in his pain — to watch and pray — was limited at best.

There will come a time with some of your low hanging fruit people where you will open yourself fully and transparently invite them into your own suffering. I've done this in many ways over the years, but there is one time when I quite literally could not have gone on without the love and ministry of my former-protege brothers. In late 2014, I had to have two urgent kidney surgeries six weeks apart. The trauma on my body was too much, and I was already dealing with some anxiety from trying family and ministry circumstances. I fell headlong into what turned out to be a 2½ year bout with severe clinical anxiety mixed with depression. It was my family and my mentees — two in particular — who were my stability and strength during those years. Like Aaron and Hur, holding up Moses' arms while Joshua and his army fought the Amalekites (Exodus 17:8-13), I had two men who stood firm under that attack and poured back into me from the reservoir I had helped to fill in them for so many years. I can never fully express how much I love them for that season of ministry.

The Second Test

As Jesus was arrested and endured that mockery of a trial, Peter had the second of his great tests. While they were still at supper together, Jesus had warned Peter that it would happen.

> *"Simon, Simon, Satan has asked to sift each of you like wheat. But I have pleaded in prayer for you, Simon, that your faith should not fail. So when you have repented and turned to me again, strengthen your brothers."*
>
> *Peter said, "Lord, I am ready to go to prison with you, and even to die with you."*
>
> *But Jesus said, "Peter, let me tell you something. Before the rooster crows tomorrow morning, you will deny three times that you even know me"* (Luke 22:31-34, New Living Translation).

Now the time had actually come. His Jesus, his rabbi — his Messiah — had been arrested. He was being tried by the religious leaders in what amounted to an illegal, nighttime trial. Peter had gone to be near his Master. And this is where the test takes place. It came out of nowhere. It was so unexpected. The test was led, of all people, by a harmless servant girl!

> *So they arrested him and led him to the high priest's home. And Peter followed at a distance. The guards lit a fire in the middle of the courtyard and sat around it, and Peter joined them there. A servant girl noticed him in the firelight and began staring at him. Finally she said, "This man was one of Jesus' followers!"*
>
> *But Peter denied it. "Woman," he said, "I don't even know him!"*
>
> *After a while someone else looked at him and said, "You must be one of them!"*
>
> *"No, man, I'm not!" Peter retorted.*
>
> *About an hour later someone else insisted, "This must be one of them, because he is a Galilean, too."*
>
> *But Peter said, "Man, I don't know what you are talking about." And immediately, while he was still speaking, the rooster crowed.*
>
> *At that moment the Lord turned and looked at Peter. Suddenly, the Lord's words flashed through Peter's mind: "Before the rooster crows tomorrow morning, you will deny three times that you even know me." And Peter left the courtyard, weeping bitterly* (Luke 22:54-62, New Living Translation).

Peter failed the test. And this was a big one. This was not a test of the depth of his faith in Jesus, it was a test of his love for Jesus. Peter failed. And he knew it to the depths of his soul. The last encounter he would have with Jesus before his death on the cross was not the Passover meal, the communion of the Lord's Table, or even a miracle on the countryside. No, his last encounter was that look on Jesus' face. The look that said both, "I warned you of this," and at the same time, "You were in my inner core, how could you deny me?" Peter wept bitterly.

Betrayal is part of the territory of reaching low hanging fruit. I'm not saying that you should expect it from everyone into which you pour your life — not at all. But there will be some — and they will often be the among your closest allies — who will turn on you.

In my own experience, Judases have been rare. I've had a few, but in each case I already knew their character by the time it happened and could see it coming. I expect betrayal from the world, and to some extent to even have Judases in my life. But it's betrayal by the Peters that knocks the wind out of my sails. I'm thankful that there have really only been three of these in my entire ministry career (to this point). One I saw the "turning" over time and could do nothing about it. The other two came completely by surprise. But in two of the cases the story was much like that of Peter. They were actually loyal, but their betrayal was borne on the wings of fear. Fear is the great underminer — even for some of the most fierce and loyal disciples.

Jesus had the privilege to know about the betrayal ahead of time. We are not told how he knew these things. Because he was living a fully human life, accepting all the limitations of humanity (except sin), he either received a clear word from the Holy Spirit, or the Father told him during one of his times of prayer. We may too see the seeds of betrayal coming — but not always. Just know it's part of the package of dealing with fallen human beings under redemption, and that it is often the result of being afraid.

The good news is that Peter's story doesn't end there. And neither should the tales of your low hanging fruit friends.

The Restoration

The gospel is the message of reconciliation. Paul says so quite directly in his second letter to the Christians at Corinth:

> *So we have stopped evaluating others from a human point of view. At one time we thought of Christ merely from a human point of view. How differently we know him now! This means that anyone who belongs to Christ has become a new person. The old life is gone; a new life has begun!*
>
> *And all of this is a gift from God, who brought us back to himself through Christ.* ***And God has given us this task of reconciling people to him.*** *For God was in Christ, reconciling the world to himself, no longer counting people's sins against them.* ***And he gave us this wonderful message of reconciliation.*** *So we are Christ's ambassadors; God is making his appeal through us. We speak for Christ when we plead, "Come back to God!"* (2 Corinthians 5:16-20, New Living Translation, **emphasis mine**)

The *primary* reason Jesus came was forgiveness. He was the living embodiment of it and he put the reconciling power of the gospel on display during his earthly ministry. Therefore, for me personally, one of the most beautiful parts of John's gospel is what happens to Peter after the resurrection. Jesus is found guilty by an illegal gathering of the Jewish Ruling Council (Luke 22:66-71). He is sentenced to death by Pontius Pilate (Luke 23:1-25). He is mercilessly beaten with a scourge — a horrible whip embedded with sharp lead teeth that would tear into the skin (Matthew 27:26; Mark 15:15; John 19:1). And he is crucified (Matthew 27:32-56). Peter is witness to it all — albeit from a distance.

No doubt, Peter is reliving the visual echo of the look on Jesus face at his third and final denial (Luke 22:61). He's a broken man. But then something incredible happens: the resurrection! Jesus is alive! He has appeared to his precious female followers who came to the grave to prepare his body for burial (Matthew 28:8-10). He had a special conversation with Mary Magdalene (John 20:11-18). Sometime after the ladies report of the empty tomb, he appeared to Peter (Luke 24:34; 1 Corinthians 15:5)! He then met two more disciples on the road to Emmaus (Luke 24:13-32). He met with his band of disciples, minus Thomas, the evening of the resurrection (Luke 24:36-49; John 20:19-23). The next week, he met with his disciples, including Thomas, and Thomas concludes that the resurrection is true (John 20:24-29)! In all, there are thirteen recorded appearances of Jesus after the resurrection in the gospel accounts. And Paul tells us in general terms that there were others (1 Corinthians 15:6-7).

The joy and exuberance his followers were feeling cannot be overstated. And yet, there is an indication that Peter may have still been grieving his final encounter with Jesus before the cross. As John concludes his gospel, he notes that some of the disciples were gathered together and Peter proclaims, "I'm going out to fish!" (John 21:3). Peter - likely with a boiling mix of emotions returns to that which he knows — to that which may be able to calm his mind – fishing. It is in the middle of this fishing trip that something beautiful happens.

> *Later, Jesus appeared again to the disciples beside the Sea of Galilee. This is how it happened. Several of the disciples were there—Simon Peter, Thomas (nicknamed the Twin), Nathanael from Cana in Galilee, the sons of Zebedee, and two other disciples.*
>
> *Simon Peter said, "I'm going fishing."*
>
> *"We'll come, too," they all said. So they went out in the boat, but they caught nothing all night.*
>
> *At dawn Jesus was standing on the beach, but the disciples couldn't see who he was. He called out, "Fellows, have you caught any fish?"*
>
> *"No," they replied.*
>
> *Then he said, "Throw out your net on the right-hand side of the boat, and you'll get some!" So they did, and they couldn't haul in the net because there were so many fish in it.*
>
> *Then the disciple Jesus loved said to Peter, "It's the Lord!" When Simon Peter heard that it was the Lord, he put on his tunic (for he had stripped for work), jumped into the water, and headed to shore. The others stayed with the boat and pulled the loaded net to the*

Building Redemptive Relationships (Part 2)

shore, for they were only about a hundred yards from shore. When they got there, they found breakfast waiting for them—fish cooking over a charcoal fire, and some bread.

"Bring some of the fish you've just caught," Jesus said. So Simon Peter went aboard and dragged the net to the shore. There were 153 large fish, and yet the net hadn't torn.

"Now come and have some breakfast!" Jesus said. None of the disciples dared to ask him, "Who are you?" They knew it was the Lord. Then Jesus served them the bread and the fish. This was the third time Jesus had appeared to his disciples since he had been raised from the dead.

After breakfast Jesus asked Simon Peter, "Simon son of John, do you love me more than these?"

"Yes, Lord," Peter replied, "you know I love you."

"Then feed my lambs," Jesus told him.

Jesus repeated the question: "Simon son of John, do you love me?"

"Yes, Lord," Peter said, "you know I love you."

"Then take care of my sheep," Jesus said.

A third time he asked him, "Simon son of John, do you love me?"

Peter was hurt that Jesus asked the question a third time. He said, "Lord, you know everything. You know that I love you."

Jesus said, "Then feed my sheep.

"I tell you the truth, when you were young, you were able to do as you liked; you dressed yourself and went wherever you wanted to go. But when you are old, you will stretch out your hands, and others will dress you and take you where you don't want to go." Jesus said this to let him know by what kind of death he would glorify God. Then Jesus told him, "Follow me."

Peter turned around and saw behind them the disciple Jesus loved—the one who had leaned over to Jesus during supper and asked, "Lord, who will betray you?" Peter asked Jesus, "What about him, Lord?"

Jesus replied, "If I want him to remain alive until I return, what is that to you? As for you, follow me" (John 21:1-22, New Living Translation).

There are many great sermons written on this passage. I love the interplay of the Greek words translated "love" into English. But my point here is a simple one: Jesus reinstates Peter. Three times Peter denied his Lord. Three times Jesus asks him if he loves him. And in response, Jesus tells Peter to get back to "feeding" those who are (and will be) Jesus' sheep. The Good Shepherd (see John 10) is recommissioning one of his three closest companions. Peter is restored. Peter is reconciled. Jesus helps Peter to know that all is forgiven and there is work to be done. And Peter now ministers from a place of deep grief immersed in the love of forgiveness.

When you experience betrayal from a low hanging fruit disciple, strive to reconcile with them. Sadly, this is not always possible. Peter's reconciliation was built upon the foundation of his godly sorrow that led to repentance (2 Corinthians 7:10). Where there is no repentance, there can be no reconciliation. But when the betrayal is borne on fear (as was Peter's), it has been my personal and mentoring experience that reconciliation is *always* a possibility. People who reacted in fear seem to always be remorseful and desperate for reconciliation. We need to give it. During the Passover meal, Jesus had already told Peter that when he turned back, he was to strengthen his brothers (Luke 22:31-32). Now Peter was ready.

Redemptive relationships are at the core of bringing low hanging fruit people into their own deep, fruit bearing walks with Christ. I hope these two chapters have given you a glimpse into what that looks like. While every relationship is unique, there are clear principles we can glean from our Savior and his own investment into others. We've spent the last few chapters building a foundation. Now we'll turn to some practical "nuts and bolts" ideas on how we can start these relationships and begin this incredible work.

PART THREE

Connecting with Low Hanging Fruit People

CHAPTER 5
Praying With People

Are any of you suffering hardships? You should pray. Are any of you happy? You should sing praises. Are any of you sick? You should call for the elders of the church to come and pray over you, anointing you with oil in the name of the Lord. Such a prayer offered in faith will heal the sick, and the Lord will make you well. And if you have committed any sins, you will be forgiven.

Confess your sins to each other and pray for each other so that you may be healed. The earnest prayer of a righteous person has great power and produces wonderful results. Elijah was as human as we are, and yet when he prayed earnestly that no rain would fall, none fell for three and a half years! Then, when he prayed again, the sky sent down rain and the earth began to yield its crops.

My dear brothers and sisters, if someone among you wanders away from the truth and is brought back, you can be sure that whoever brings the sinner back from wandering will save that person from death and bring about the forgiveness of many sins
(James 5:13-20, New Living Translation).

LOW HANGING FRUIT

Over the last decade or so, I have been holding myself to a promise. I tend to have a lot of things happening in my life simultaneously. As a result, there is a lot of stuff taking up real estate in my mind and memory. I find that I have very good intentions about a lot of things, but my follow-through is hampered by my memory and my busyness. An area where I feel a particular conviction about this is prayer. To combat this, I made a change. Instead of telling people I would pray for them when a need arose, I began asking them if I could pray WITH them — right there and then. Not only does this help with being faithful to actually pray for people, but it also *engages* them spiritually. It's turned out to be a big deal. One of the most important outcomes of this change is that I have started identifying low hanging fruit people as we connect in those prayers.

Some of you reading this may be experiencing a little apprehension about where this chapter is taking us. Is he going to suggest that I pray with people? The answer is yes. I understand that many people are afraid to pray out loud. I understand that even many churchgoers have not taken regular opportunities to pray with people in need. But if we are serious about partnering with the Holy Spirit to reach low the hanging fruit people around us, then we need to be like the early church and regain our devotion to prayer (see Chapter 1). If you have never had anyone teach you about the many facets of prayer, then that is the place to start. But more than just getting a good book on how to pray — find a mature brother or sister in Christ and start practicing it. You will learn more by actually praying than by reading about it. And if you can find a mentor who already has a great track record in answered prayer, all the better.

Let's begin with what I've found is a radical idea for many people: the primary purpose of prayer is not to get results. Let that sink in for a moment. The bible certainly teaches us to pray when we have needs, and to expect our loving Abba Father to respond. But I submit that this should not be our primary motivation for prayer. We are told that Jesus often withdrew from the crowds and the noise to pray (Luke 5:16). What do you think he was doing all those times he stepped away? Did he take a "laundry list" of needs to present to his Heavenly Father? Or do you think that expressing needs and asking about plans was only a small part of what he was doing? Could it be that his primary motivation for these regular retreats was simply to spend time with his Dad?

Look, the Father knows what we need before we ask him. Jesus says,

> *But when you pray, go away by yourself, shut the door behind you, and pray to your Father in private. Then your Father, who sees everything, will reward you.*
>
> *"When you pray, don't babble on and on as the Gentiles do. They think their prayers are answered merely by repeating their words again and again. Don't be like them, for your Father knows exactly what you need even before you ask him!* (Matthew 6:6-8, New Living Translation).

In fact, this passage is the precursor to Jesus' whole teaching on prayer to his disciples — which we call the Lord's Prayer. If this is the model we are to use, then making requests is only a portion of prayer's purpose. Jesus tells us to:

> *Pray like this:*
> *Our Father in heaven,*
> *may your name be kept holy.*
> *May your Kingdom come soon.*
> *May your will be done on earth,*
> *as it is in heaven.*
> *Give us today the food we need,*
> *and forgive us our sins,*
> *as we have forgiven those who sin against us.*
> *And don't let us yield to temptation,*
> *but rescue us from the evil one.*
> (Matthew 6:9-13, New Living Translation)

Before a single request is made, Jesus teaches us to get everything else in order. Think of it this way:

- *Our Father in heaven* - we start with the relationship we have with God as his beloved, redeemed sons and daughters in Jesus.
- *May your name be kept holy* - we worship, placing ourselves in the proper prayer posture before our holy God.
- *May your Kingdom come soon* - we surrender afresh to his rule and reign (the meaning of the word 'Kingdom' here), and ask that it fully extend throughout the earth.
- *May your will be done* - if we've truly surrendered to his rule and reign, then this makes sense — we purpose to do what he asks of us. And there's a qualifier...
- *On earth as it is in heaven* - we pray to be as faithful and as obedient here on earth as the holy angels are around his throne.
- *Give us today the food we need* - only after we realign our relationship with him do we begin to make requests. But notice that even the request is only for *today*. We must come back to him *daily*, remaining *dependent* on Him.
- *Forgive us our sins* - then we go back to our relationship with Him. And even this request is qualified...
- *As we have forgiven those who sin against us* - Jesus actually teaches us to ask God to forgive us in the same way we are forgiving others.
- *And don't let us yield to temptation* - help us overcome our flesh with its propensity to sin and to cave to temptation.
- *Rescue us from the evil one* - a prayer for very real protection from the enemy of our souls.

It's not that we don't make requests in prayer, but that the majority of our praying is about our relationship with the Father. How different this kind of praying is! But doesn't it make sense? If the only time I talked with my wife was when I wanted something from her, how would our relationship be? I can tell you she would not be happy if every time I approached her I had a list of things I wanted her to do for me. God does not want that either. He desires intimacy. He loves to lavish answers to our prayers, but he is more concerned with our hearts than our prayer lists. When this kind of praying is our personal, daily routine, then stepping out in faith to pray with others is simply an extension of that prayer life.

Prayer Offered in Faith

Keep this perspective: praying with others about their needs is not an event in and of itself, but it is simply a part of the ongoing conversation you are already having with your Heavenly Father all day, every day (1 Thessalonians 5:17). And as people experience your prayer relationship with your Father, they will see that it is not a "religious thing" but is genuine faith. The Holy Spirit will use this to woo low hanging fruit people. Let's talk about what this looks like.

We Faithfully Pray in All Circumstances

When you connect with someone with whom you will be praying, it doesn't matter what their need is. Prayer should always be our first step. Even when we feel overwhelmed by their situation and cannot fathom the best way to pray, we pray — and we're promised that the Holy Spirit will help us. Paul tells us,

> *...The Holy Spirit helps us in our weakness. For example, we don't know what God wants us to pray for. But the Holy Spirit prays for us with groanings that cannot be expressed in words. And the Father who knows all hearts knows what the Spirit is saying, for the Spirit pleads for us believers in harmony with God's own will. And we know that God causes everything to work together for the good of those who love God and are called according to his purpose for them* (Romans 8:26-28, New Living Translation).

Because we know we are God's precious, beloved and redeemed children in Jesus, we can truly live with great confidence. But be careful here: our confidence is not in a particular answer to prayer, but in God Himself. When my kids were little and had a crisis or were afraid, they didn't necessarily have confidence that a situation would end in a certain way. They just knew that if Daddy was there, they would be safe and protected. It's the same for us. We can have joy and confidence in every situation because we know that our loving Father is there with us.

Rejoice in our confident hope. Be patient in trouble, and keep on praying (Romans 12:12, New Living Translation).

It's not hard to pray with and for people consistently if your own prayer conversation with God is ongoing. Your prayer is not contingent on a particular outcome, but on the love and faithfulness of your Father.

Pray in the Spirit at all times and on every occasion. Stay alert and be persistent in your prayers for all believers everywhere (Ephesians 6:18, New Living Translation).

As we pray *with* people, our own faith and confidence affects them. And as the Holy Spirit continues his work in their hearts, we will begin to see his hand.

Always be joyful. Never stop praying. Be thankful in all circumstances, for this is God's will for you who belong to Christ Jesus.

Do not stifle the Holy Spirit (1 Thessalonians 5:16-19, New Living Translation).

We pray the full gamut of prayer as we pray with people (see Chapter 1) — ongoing conversation with the Father, urgent pleas, stand-in-the-gap intercession, and always thanksgiving and praise. Again, the Spirit will use such a prayer relationship with God to woo low hanging fruit people.

> *I urge you, first of all, to pray for all people. Ask God to help them; intercede on their behalf, and give thanks for them. Pray this way for kings and all who are in authority so that we can live peaceful and quiet lives marked by godliness and dignity. This is good and pleases God our Savior, who wants everyone to be saved and to understand the truth* (1 Timothy 2:1-4, New Living Translation).

We engage in prayer for all kinds of trouble.

As Jesus' half brother James writes about prayer in his letter to the church, he begins with an important question:

"Are any of you suffering hardships? You should pray" (James 5:13, New Living Translation).

The Greek word he uses is a general term that covers all kinds of suffering and misfortune. It doesn't matter what kind of trouble someone is having, your praying with them is always the best first step.

Paul teaches the Roman Christians this principle in their relationship with him. We know that Paul suffered much for his apostleship. He now *invites* the believers in Rome to join him in his suffering through prayer.

Dear brothers and sisters, I urge you in the name of our Lord Jesus Christ to join in my struggle by praying to God for me. Do this because of your love for me, given to you by the Holy Spirit (Romans 15:30, New Living Translation).

This is precisely what we do with those with whom we pray. We effectively *join them* in their suffering — in their trouble. Our efforts are an expression of genuine Christian love, driven by the Holy Spirit, and they become a significant factor in the wooing of low hanging fruit people.

We offer praise for all kinds of blessings.

Keep in mind that prayer is not just for trouble. It is also for rejoicing! James also says,

"Are any of you happy? You should sing praises" (James 5:13, New Living Translation).

People seem to expect Christians to offer prayer in times of crisis. But my experience is that they are surprised when we offer to pray or praise God with them in times of blessing.

In his second letter to the church at Corinth, Paul thanks them because many people are giving thanks for answered prayers.

> *And [God] did rescue us from mortal danger, and he will rescue us again. We have placed our confidence in him, and he will continue to rescue us. And you are helping us by praying for us. Then many people will give thanks because God has graciously answered so many prayers for our safety* (2 Corinthians 1:10-11, New Living Translation).

Don't miss this point: prayerfully praising and rejoicing with people is just as powerful a witness as praying for their hardships.

We engage in concerted prayer for healing and deliverance.

Prayer for healing is a pretty common occurrence. Every believer has experience asking God to heal someone. But many Christians report a frustrating lack of *answers* to those prayers. I can't speak to every person's lack of answered prayer, but I can explain some trends that I think are contributing factors.

First, way too many people pray only a quick, pointed prayer for someone's situation. I'm not saying that any prayer is ineffectual, but I would submit to you that all prayer needs to be fruit of our ongoing prayer conversation with the Father. Consistent prayer every day in relationship with God breeds a more persistent prayer for needs that arise throughout the day. It is often not a quick, singular prayer that brings about a miraculous response, but fervent and ongoing prayer rooted in a deep, existing prayer foundation.

Do you remember the time when Jesus' disciples could not cast a demon out of a little boy? Jesus was able to deliver the boy and then used the "debrief" of that situation to teach his disciples a deeper lesson (see Mark 9:14-29). His disciples were bothered that they could not do it.

> *Afterward, when Jesus was alone in the house with his disciples, they asked him, "Why couldn't we cast out that evil spirit?"*
>
> *Jesus replied, "This kind can be cast out only by prayer"* (Mark 9:28-29, New Living Translation).

"This kind can be cast out only by prayer." And some manuscripts say "...only by prayer and fasting." What Jesus is describing here is a concerted and persistent kind of prayer. A quick, singular prayer won't cut it. And so we enter into fervent prayer.

Second, too many Christians today do not pray in *concert* with others. Agreement in prayer with other believers is a powerful thing! Jesus says to his followers:

> *"I also tell you this: If two of you agree here on earth concerning anything you ask, my Father in heaven will do it for you. For where two or three gather together as my followers, I am there among them"* (Matthew 18:19-20, New Living Translation).

I think it's also important here that James instructs us to call upon the elders in these situations.

> *Are any of you sick? You should call for the elders of the church to come and pray over you, anointing you with oil in the name of the Lord. Such a prayer offered in faith will heal the sick, and the Lord will make you well. And if you have committed any sins, you will be forgiven* (James 5:14-15, New Living Translation).

The elders of a church should be among the most mature and fruitful believers in the body. Elders are to be growing in the spiritual maturity and Christlike character traits listed by Paul in 1 Timothy 3:1-7. It makes sense to include them in this kind of fervent and persistent praying — they are supposed to be those with the strongest faith and the most experienced when it comes to such matters. This is why they are chosen to be elders.

Healing and deliverance prayer is often hard work. Do not give up. But when low hanging fruit people experience your love and devotion through such prayer, the Holy Spirit can use that to take them deeper in their own burgeoning faith walk.

We practice confession and forgiveness as a prerequisite.

This should be no surprise to the believer who is consistent in their prayer relationship with the Father. Jesus teaches us that asking for forgiveness and granting forgiveness are at the very heart of both the Christian Faith and our prayer life:

> *...And forgive us our sins,*
> *as we have forgiven those who sin against us...*

> *"If you forgive those who sin against you, your heavenly Father will forgive you. But if you refuse to forgive others, your Father will not forgive your sins* (Matthew 6:12, 14-15, New Living Translation).

Since we know that, for the children of God down through the ages, their sin is the biggest obstacle in their prayer life, it makes perfect sense that this should remain a top priority as we pray for ourselves and with other people.

> *Listen! The Lord's arm is not too weak to save you,*
> *nor is his ear too deaf to hear you call.*
> *It's your sins that have cut you off from God.*
> *Because of your sins, he has turned away*
> *and will not listen anymore* (Isaiah 59:1-2, New Living Translation).

> *Come and listen, all you who fear God,*
> *and I will tell you what he did for me.*
> *For I cried out to him for help,*
> *praising him as I spoke.*
> *If I had not confessed the sin in my heart,*
> *the Lord would not have listened.*
> *But God did listen!*
> *He paid attention to my prayer.*
> *Praise God, who did not ignore my prayer*
> *or withdraw his unfailing love from me*
> (Psalm 66:16-20, New Living Translation).

It is no mistake that James links confession of sin with the fervent prayer of the elders.

> *Are any of you sick? You should call for the elders of the church to come and pray over you, anointing you with oil in the name of the*

Lord. Such a prayer offered in faith will heal the sick, and the Lord will make you well. And if you have committed any sins, you will be forgiven.

Confess your sins to each other and pray for each other so that you may be healed. The earnest prayer of a righteous person has great power and produces wonderful results (James 5:14-16, New Living Translation).

As we pray with low hanging fruit people about their own needs, we need to put this confession and forgiveness on display to them while we live it out in our own lives. Yet this is a challenge. Christians, of all people, should be the most trustworthy. But this is not the case. Many a church member has experienced the betrayal of gossip and other breaches of confidence at the hands of fellow believers. Precious few people within local churches would confess their sin to one another today. You can imagine, therefore, how hard it would be to do so outside of the church family.

In my opinion, this may be one of the biggest hindrances to our prayers — corporate and personal — in the Western church. But there are still ways we can begin this process with low hanging fruit people. First, if we have said or done something to hurt or offend them (even in the past), we can appropriately confess it as sinful and ask them for their forgiveness. This is often a very powerful exercise. We may need to explain confession's relationship to prayer — that we don't want anything to hinder our prayer efforts. Second, we can counsel them about confession and forgiveness in their own lives. If they have not yet trusted Christ, it will likely be new to them. But if the Holy Spirit is already preparing their hearts, you might be amazed at how interested they are to learn more. Start with showing them how to quietly confess sin to God on their own. Then show them what it looks like to confess to someone they have wronged. They may or may not practice it with you at that moment, but trust that the Holy Spirit will now add that part of the conversation to his arsenal. I've had people come back to me later after "percolating" on the topic for a few days. Sometimes they'll ask for clarification. But other times they'll ask for help actually doing it. It is then you'll realize the fruit is ripening.

We follow biblical examples before us.

I love that James gives us the example of Elijah right in the middle of his short teaching on prayer.

> *Elijah was as human as we are, and yet when he prayed earnestly that no rain would fall, none fell for three and a half years! Then, when he prayed again, the sky sent down rain and the earth began to yield its crops* (James 5:17-18, New Living Translation).

The whole story of Elijah's prayer is in 1 Kings 17 & 18. I've been on Mount Carmel. I've seen the area where Elijah did his ministry. The Roman Catholic Church has erected a monument to Elijah on the top of the mountain. I can remember standing there looking at that statue thinking what a "superhuman" he seemed to be. And then our Messianic guide turned us to these very verses. Isn't it wonderful that James begins his commentary on Elijah's example with the words, "Elijah was as human as we are..."?

It wasn't that Elijah was superhuman or even special — it was that he was in a right relationship with God and he prayed *earnestly* (James 5:17). He is an example that every one of us can follow.

We partner with the Holy Spirit to woo people to the truth.

James ends his letter with a precious reminder to all who would read it.

> *My dear brothers and sisters, if someone among you wanders away from the truth and is brought back, you can be sure that whoever brings the sinner back from wandering will save that person from death and bring about the forgiveness of many sins* (James 5:19-20, New Living Translation).

Ultimately, you and I are truth bearers. If we are devoted followers of Jesus, then we are devoted followers of the Truth (with a capital "T") because truth is not just propositional, Truth is a Person (see John 14:6). It is truth from which the low hanging fruit people have been blinded. Paul writes,

> *If the Good News we preach is hidden behind a veil, it is hidden only from people who are perishing. Satan, who is the god of this world, has blinded the minds of those who don't believe. They are unable to see the glorious light of the Good News. They don't understand this message about the glory of Christ, who is the exact likeness of God* (2 Corinthians 4:4, New Living Translation).

There is no need to get frustrated with those for whom the Holy Spirit has not yet completed his work. They *cannot* see spiritual truth as true. Describing this dilemma, Paul writes,

> *When we tell you these things, we do not use words that come from human wisdom. Instead, we speak words given to us by the Spirit, using the Spirit's words to explain spiritual truths. But people who aren't spiritual can't receive these truths from God's Spirit. It all sounds foolish to them and they can't understand it, for only those who are spiritual can understand what the Spirit means* (1 Corinthians 2:13-14, New Living Translation).

This is a big reason why witnessing, evangelism and other gospel-based ministries are fruitless with people who are not yet low hanging fruit. They have not yet responded to the enlightening work of the Holy Spirit and real, spiritual truth is still absolute foolishness to them. They are deceived and fall more deeply in love with their deception every day. They actually pursue it! Paul warns his son-in-the-faith Timothy about such people.

> *For a time is coming when people will no longer listen to sound and wholesome teaching. They will follow their own desires and will look for teachers who will tell them whatever their itching ears want to hear. They will reject the truth and chase after myths* (2 Timothy 4:3-4, New Living Translation).

When you and I actively partner with the Holy Spirit in his work, at some point low hanging fruit people begin to see the truth for themselves and it becomes instantly life-giving to them. They get excited about it. They become inquisitive. They get an insatiable appetite for it. The Bible goes from being a nice book of "moral" teaching but not much personal significance, to the very Word of God. The words on its pages grab their eyes and they love what they are beginning to now understand.

This kind of praying is part of the larger mission.

Praying with people opens all kinds of opportunities to identify low hanging fruit. The praying itself is a direct partnership with the Holy Spirit in that work. The whole point of this book is to help us become better and more intentional partners — and this kind of praying is a critical tool the Father has given us, in part, for that purpose.

It starts as we grow in our own prayer faithfulness and consistency. If you don't have a daily prayer relationship with the Father as a foundation, then that's where you need to focus first. Remember, prayer's primary purpose is to grow your relationship with the Father, not to get what you want. But as you grow in your daily praying, then you need to make yourselves aware of the circumstances of those around you. You need to have conversations with people employing a listening ear. If people are resistant, then they are likely not ready. But as people share their troubles, the next step is to ask them if you can pray with them about those things. Don't forget that you should also ask if you can pray a prayer of praise for any blessings they report! Pray with people for healing and deliverance — whether it is for them personally or someone they love. Tell them you will continue to be persistent (fervent) in that praying — and then be so! Check back with them often to see how God might be responding.

If they are low hanging fruit people, it is likely that your relationship with them will grow. They may even show signs of curiosity about Jesus and spiritual things. As that happens, help them understand what sin is — both against God and against other people. Show them what the Bible says about sin's impact. And when you feel the nudge of the Spirit to go deeper, begin explaining the critical importance of confession and forgiveness. Make sure you are building a trustworthy relationship where it can take place. And all along the way, graciously show them the truth of scripture. The Holy Spirit will take that and build on it, with the hopeful end that they become believers themselves.

So as we close out this chapter, stop and pray. Who in your life *right now* needs you to offer such prayer? Will you do it?

CHAPTER 6
Starting Spiritual Conversations

On the Sabbath we went a little way outside the city to a riverbank, where we thought people would be meeting for prayer, and we sat down to speak with some women who had gathered there. One of them was Lydia from Thyatira, a merchant of expensive purple cloth, who worshiped God. As she listened to us, the Lord opened her heart, and she accepted what Paul was saying. She and her household were baptized, and she asked us to be her guests. "If you agree that I am a true believer in the Lord," she said, "come and stay at my home." And she urged us until we agreed (Acts 16:13-15, New Living Translation).

You may or may not have noticed, but we have already given multiple biblical examples in previous chapters of conversations being lovingly guided toward spiritual things and ultimately to the gospel. The passage above about Paul's first connection with Lydia is a classic — and Lydia effectively became a church planter as a result, with the Philippian Church being established right in her own home. It is clear that the Holy Spirit had been tilling the soil of her heart long before she ever met Paul at the riverbank.

A spiritual conversation is a dialogue with someone, usually already a friend, a family member, a neighbor, a co-worker, or another existing relationship, that leads them to an encounter with Jesus. Sometimes it leads quickly to salvation, but not always. The goal is the encounter with Jesus — remember that it's the Holy Spirit's job to lead people across the line of conversion because we cannot see into their hearts. Jesus tells us,

> *And when [the Holy Spirit] comes, he will convict the world of its sin, and of God's righteousness, and of the coming judgment* (John 16:8, New Living Translation).

In his seminal work, *What's Gone Wrong with the Harvest*, Jim Engle helps us see that the movement to faith in Christ is not an event but a journey. And for some people, it's an incremental "inching" along a growing faith pathway that he describes in his Engle Scale of Evangelism.[6] Even after a person surrenders their lives to Jesus as King and Savior, the journey continues. But now they will be asking more and deeper spiritual questions and seeking to grow on their own.

One of the best examples of a new spiritual conversation is Jesus' encounter with the Samaritan woman at Jacob's well.

> *Jesus knew the Pharisees had heard that he was baptizing and making more disciples than John (though Jesus himself didn't baptize them—his disciples did). So he left Judea and returned to Galilee.*
>
> *He had to go through Samaria on the way. Eventually he came to the Samaritan village of Sychar, near the field that Jacob gave to his son Joseph. Jacob's well was there; and Jesus, tired from the long walk, sat wearily beside the well about noontime. Soon a Samaritan woman came to draw water, and Jesus said to her, "Please give me a drink." He was alone at the time because his disciples had gone into the village to buy some food.*
>
> *The woman was surprised, for Jews refuse to have anything to do with Samaritans. She said to Jesus, "You are a Jew, and I am a Samaritan woman. Why are you asking me for a drink?"*

---

6 James F. Engle and Wilbert Norton, *What's Gone Wrong with the Harvest: A Communication Strategy for the Church and World Evangelism*, Grand Rapids: Zondervan Publishing House, 1975.

Jesus replied, "If you only knew the gift God has for you and who you are speaking to, you would ask me, and I would give you living water."

"But sir, you don't have a rope or a bucket," she said, "and this well is very deep. Where would you get this living water? And besides, do you think you're greater than our ancestor Jacob, who gave us this well? How can you offer better water than he and his sons and his animals enjoyed?"

Jesus replied, "Anyone who drinks this water will soon become thirsty again. But those who drink the water I give will never be thirsty again. It becomes a fresh, bubbling spring within them, giving them eternal life."

"Please, sir," the woman said, "give me this water! Then I'll never be thirsty again, and I won't have to come here to get water."

"Go and get your husband," Jesus told her.

"I don't have a husband," the woman replied.

Jesus said, "You're right! You don't have a husband—for you have had five husbands, and you aren't even married to the man you're living with now. You certainly spoke the truth!"

"Sir," the woman said, "you must be a prophet. So tell me, why is it that you Jews insist that Jerusalem is the only place of worship, while we Samaritans claim it is here at Mount Gerizim, where our ancestors worshiped?"

Jesus replied, "Believe me, dear woman, the time is coming when it will no longer matter whether you worship the Father on this mountain or in Jerusalem. You Samaritans know very little about the one you worship, while we Jews know all about him, for salvation comes through the Jews. But the time is coming—indeed it's here now—when true worshipers will worship the Father in spirit and in truth. The Father is looking for those who will worship him that way. For God is Spirit, so those who worship him must worship in spirit and in truth."

The woman said, "I know the Messiah is coming—the one who is called Christ. When he comes, he will explain everything to us."

Then Jesus told her, "I Am the Messiah!" (John 4:1-26, New Living Translation).

The characteristics of Jesus' conversation with this woman are very helpful to us.

Jesus' Conversation Has Intentionality

I find it interesting that the passage tells us that Jesus *had* to go through Samaria. While it may have been the shortest route, it is a well-known fact that most good Jews would voluntarily take long routes around Samaria to avoid encountering any Samaritans. There was historic prejudice and hatred between them. For routing reasons, Jesus would not have had to go through Samaria. So I believe there was something else here. Perhaps he was aware of his upcoming conversation with this woman? Maybe he had received specific instructions from his Father in prayer? We don't know, but he clearly intended to take that specific route.

His conversation with the Samaritan woman is also borne on the wings of intentionality. He's in a place where no good Jew (let alone a rabbi) would be found. He strikes up a conversation with a Samaritan woman, which simply was not done. And then he goes directly for her heart. We too must make spiritual conversations with intentionality. In some cases, we're simply chatting normally with a friend or colleague and we steer it toward spiritual things. But in other cases, we will start a conversation for the express purpose of guiding someone to an encounter with Jesus.

Jesus' Conversation Begins with Mundane Dialog

It's a simple request. "Please give me a drink..." Granted, a rabbi asking a Samaritan for a drink would have been highly unusual in and of itself, but the request was not earth shattering. It's amazing how many spiritual conversations begin with the mundane. You may be talking about a common experience. You may be discussing family stuff. You might even be talking about the weather! But the mundane is the gateway to a deeper conversational pathway. It allows for an initial level of trust — and it also gives the Holy Spirit time to prime the pump of their heart.

My dear friend Steven Barr, Executive Director and Pastor of Cast Member Church[7] which ministers to cast members of the Walt Disney Parks around the world, has three great questions he uses to initiate

---

[7] You can learn more about Cast Member Church on their website at www.castmemberchurch.com.

spiritual conversations with people. They are simple, and yet they provide both vital information and open the heart to a deeper conversation because they help people see that we are genuinely interested in their personal story.

- *Question #1: What brought you to Disney?* - Right off the bat you learn something about their background, even if it's just the pathway that brought them to work in the parks.
- *Question #2: What is your favorite part about working for Disney?* - With this next question, you learn something current about their heart and their passion.
- *Question #3: How are you going to use what you are learning here at Disney for the future?* - The final question gives you a glimpse into their hopes and dreams for the future.

With these three questions, and genuine listening to their respective responses, you gain a lot of insight into a person's life that can become a springboard for a deeper and more meaningful spiritual conversation. And what's so masterful is that Steven's "Three Questions" can be contextualized for literally any situation. He's used them in restaurants, in meetings and even standing in line at the grocery checkout!

What seems like mundane conversation is actually intentional and critical. This makes it much easier to begin turning the dialogue toward an encounter with Jesus.

Jesus Turns the Conversation Toward Spiritual Things

Now, of course, Jesus is masterful at this, but did you catch what he does next? He makes a statement that is intended to stir the woman's curiosity: *"If you only knew the gift God has for you and who you are speaking to, you would ask me, and I would give you living water."* There is a little shock value, but even moreso, the statement likely invokes several questions:

"Who are YOU?"

"What is this gift of which you speak?"

"What is this 'living water'?"

Any of these kinds of questions can become a pathway for Jesus to draw her deeper. And that's exactly what happens.

As we employ similar ways with people, we need to make sure we remain prayerfully sensitive to the Holy Spirit's leading. Remember, only the Spirit knows if they are ready for a deeper conversation. We watch for opportunities to tweak the person's interest. We continue to look for signs that they are low hanging fruit. And, especially if they start asking spiritual questions (as the Samaritan woman does), we take them a little deeper. She asks Jesus if he is greater than Jacob. The door opens a little wider.

Jesus Draws the Woman Toward the Gospel

While it is clear that the woman is thinking in the natural while Jesus is talking about the spiritual, the conversation does stir a desire in her.

> *Jesus replied, "Anyone who drinks this water will soon become thirsty again. But those who drink the water I give will never be thirsty again. It becomes a fresh, bubbling spring within them, giving them eternal life."*
>
> *"Please, sir," the woman said, "give me this water! Then I'll never be thirsty again, and I won't have to come here to get water"* (John 4:13-14, New Living Translation).

As the Spirit leads, use what you've learned thus far in your conversation to plant a gospel seed. They might have opened the door by talking about an issue of pain or faith — even a previous bad experience with another Christian. Or you might be led to be more direct — something like, "Tell me about your view of God," or "Why do you think God put you on this earth?" But in all things, rely on the Holy Spirit. Slow down when he tells you to slow down. Take another step forward when he tells you to go further. Trust him. Being prepared to woo people toward the gospel should be on our heart in *every* conversation. This seems so irregular today, but it should be our standard operating procedure.

Jesus Challenges Her Current Understanding

In the passage above, the Samaritan woman now challenges Jesus about the proper place of worship. Whether this is what she had been taught or it is what she has gathered on her own about God, what she says shows Jesus that her understanding of God, worship and the Messiah are all misaligned. Notice that Jesus does not tell her she is wrong (at least not directly). Instead, he guides her toward a better, truer understanding.

You and I must remain active students of God's word and his works. This is important because it hones our own faith and understanding. It keeps us doctrinally sharp so that we too can identify misaligned beliefs when we hear them and lovingly, gently bring alignment to the conversation. Again, follow the Spirit. Humility is key! We never bring alignment and correction to show how much we know, but to give the low hanging fruit person to whom we're talking a truth encounter with Jesus. And that's precisely what Jesus does here.

Jesus Points Her to the Truth

Remember, truth is not just a proposition — Truth is a Person. It's Jesus (John 14:6). The Pharisees studied the Scriptures propositionally, but they still missed their Messiah, Truth himself. Jesus confronts them,

> *"You search the Scriptures because you think they give you eternal life. But the Scriptures point to me! Yet you refuse to come to me to receive this life"* (John 5:39-40, New Living Translation).

Jesus makes it clear that he is the Messiah — he is the one for whom she has been looking:

> *The woman said, "I know the Messiah is coming—the one who is called Christ. When he comes, he will explain everything to us."*
>
> *Then Jesus told her, "I Am the Messiah!"* (John 4:25-26, New Living Translation).

Interestingly, Jesus' first admission that he is the Messiah is not to the Jews, but to this Samaritan woman! The bottom line is that Jesus introduces the

Samaritan woman to *himself.* And we must do the same. The ultimate end of our conversations is to woo people to encounter Jesus as the answer — *their* answer.

One Response Turns to Many

Notice that the woman, now stirred and largely convinced, goes and begins to tell others what she has experienced. When we start spiritual conversations with low hanging fruit people, such conversations will nearly always have far reaching repercussions. One successful spiritual conversation can bear fruit on many levels. In this case, as we read the rest of the story, the whole town comes out to meet Jesus!

> *Many Samaritans from the village believed in Jesus because the woman had said, "He told me everything I ever did!" When they came out to see him, they begged him to stay in their village. So he stayed for two days, long enough for many more to hear his message and believe. Then they said to the woman, "Now we believe, not just because of what you told us, but because we have heard him ourselves. Now we know that he is indeed the Savior of the world"* (John 4:39-42, New Living Translation).

Practical Application

There are many great resources available today on the topic of starting really good spiritual conversations. Two of my favorites are *Spiritual Conversations: Creating and Sustaining Them Without Being a Jerk* by Gary Rohrmayer[8] and *Evangelism Made Slightly Less Difficult: How to Interest People Who Aren't Interested* by Nick Pollard.[9] And there is a great small group study that is also incredibly helpful on this topic, *Activating God Space: Equipping Your People to Be the Church in Everyday Life*[10]

---

8 Gary Rohrmayer, *Spiritual Conversations: Creating and Sustaining Them Without Being a Jerk*, St. Charles IL: ChurchSmart Resources, 2010.

9 Nick Pollard, *Evangelism Made Slightly Less Difficult: How to Interest People Who Aren't Interested*, Downers Grove IL: IVP Books, 1997.

10 *Activating God Space Kit,* Loveland CO: Group Publishing, 2016.

by Group Publishing, based upon the book by Doug Pollock.[11] I have used all of these resources and more in my own ministry, training people how to start really good and appropriate spiritual conversations.

As we close out this chapter, I'd like to turn now to a process I've adapted from a practical article by Floyd Schneider, *How to Turn A Conversation to Spiritual Things*.[12] Schneider teaches four simple stages to keep in mind as we lovingly guide our low hanging fruit friends toward a spiritual conversation.

1. Surface Talk - we begin the conversation with surface talk. Topics might include sports, the weather, the Marvel superhero universe — really anything light that is universal to most people.

2. Personal Talk - After allowing surface talk to prime the pump as it were, and if the person is beginning to open up, gently move the conversation to a more personal level. Personal talk may be initiated with questions about family, careers or other interests — especially any interests we have in common. If there is noticeable openness to keep the conversation going, then initiate a non-threatening religious question or two. Granted, this is easier for me because I'm a pastor. Personal talk nearly always leads to the person asking what I do for a living. But even for non-pastors, it can be something as simple as, "Read any good books lately?" To which I can eventually contribute that I'm reading a really good book by [fill in the author of my current Christian text].

3. Religious Talk - Religious talk is to be very general in nature. Even if they begin asking me specific questions about my own ministry, I try to keep the conversation a little superficial at first. We might talk about religion in general, or Christianity more specifically. I might begin to ask them about their own church experience. I might ask about church activities they've enjoyed. Don't be surprised if, at this stage,

---

11   Doug Pollock, *God Space: Where Spiritual Conversations Happen Naturally,* Citrus Heights CA: LifeTree Books, 2009.

12   Floyd Schneider, *How to Turn a Conversation to Spiritual Things,* online, CrossWalk.Com, 29 May 2002.

you start to hear what they *don't* like about the Church. Listen without explanation or defense. At an appropriate time you might contribute something like, "I don't like that either."

4. Spiritual Talk - If the conversation is going well with religious talk, it's very easy to slide into an authentic spiritual conversation. In fact, if they have not pushed back by this point, it's possible they may even be showing some signs of genuine spiritual interest. If so, you now know they are a low hanging fruit person! Appropriate to the topics at hand, share some of your own spiritual journey. Tell them what Christ has done for you. Remain sensitive to the Holy Spirit about sharing the gospel, but if you get to this point their heart is likely ready. Invite them to join you in a bible study. Invite them to worship — but remember that people today are more likely to join you for a small group in someone's home than a worship service at first. Be gracious if they decline.

In today's world, people tend to be confused, scared or hurting more than ever. Our world has been through a lot — a pandemic, economic upheaval that was catastrophic to so many, social unrest, and ongoing nastiness in politics. Be led of the Spirit, but know that many today are actually yearning for answers and relief. Our religion isn't the answer: our Jesus is. Guiding people toward an encounter with Christ is our goal. Let him use you. You might just be in the right place and time to witness a soul experience Jesus' redemption for the very first time.

CHAPTER 7

Showing Jesus' Love

Therefore, since God in his mercy has given us this new way, we never give up. We reject all shameful deeds and underhanded methods. We don't try to trick anyone or distort the word of God. We tell the truth before God, and all who are honest know this.

If the Good News we preach is hidden behind a veil, it is hidden only from people who are perishing. Satan, who is the god of this world, has blinded the minds of those who don't believe. They are unable to see the glorious light of the Good News. They don't understand this message about the glory of Christ, who is the exact likeness of God.

You see, we don't go around preaching about ourselves. We preach that Jesus Christ is Lord, and we ourselves are your servants for Jesus' sake. For God, who said, "Let there be light in the darkness," has made this light shine in our hearts so we could know the glory of God that is seen in the face of Jesus Christ. (2 Corinthians 4:1-6, New Living Translation)

There are many ways to show Jesus' love, but chief among them are service and sacrifice. These two are closely related — and Jesus is our example.

LOW HANGING FRUIT

> *So Jesus called them together and said, "You know that the rulers in this world lord it over their people, and officials flaunt their authority over those under them. But among you it will be different. Whoever wants to be a leader among you must be your servant, and whoever wants to be first among you must be the slave of everyone else. For even the Son of Man came not to be served but to serve others and to give his life as a ransom for many"* (Mark 10:42-45, New Living Translation).

This is one of the most beloved teachings by our Savior. It describes his own heart in the midst of his mission to save humanity. It also teaches us about our hearts as we partner with him.

One of the most fruitful ways to connect with and identify low hanging fruit people is through service, especially sacrificial service. This is because they are already responding to the work of the Holy Spirit within them. Their hearts will take notice — even resonate with — acts of Christlike service. Such service is one of the greatest weapons in our spiritual arsenal against the work of the enemy.

Showing Jesus' love to people falls on a wide spectrum. It can be simple acts of kindness, or it can be personally costly and challenging. I have heard all kinds of stories over the years of how such Christlike service connects Christians with low hanging fruit people. A 12-year-old feels the "twinge" of the Holy Spirit to bless his elderly neighbor and volunteers to mow his grass all summer — an act that ultimately led to that neighbor becoming like family and growing in faith during his golden years. A childless couple decides to adopt and initially thinks they got more than they bargained for — adopting several siblings to keep them together, all who now as adults are serving the Lord. A lady's friendly conversation at McDonalds with a lonely woman turns into a friendship where that woman comes to Christ. The stories are many and varied, but they all beautifully display how the Holy Spirit can use an act of service to connect us with a new low hanging fruit friend.

Jesus shows us the heart of a servant and calls us to do likewise. As he writes his second letter to the Christians at Corinth, the Apostle Paul gives us insight into how to carry that service out, as well as how the enemy of our souls opposes us.

Therefore, since God in his mercy has given us this new way, we never give up. We reject all shameful deeds and underhanded methods. We don't try to trick anyone or distort the word of God. We tell the truth before God, and all who are honest know this.

If the Good News we preach is hidden behind a veil, it is hidden only from people who are perishing. Satan, who is the god of this world, has blinded the minds of those who don't believe. They are unable to see the glorious light of the Good News. They don't understand this message about the glory of Christ, who is the exact likeness of God.

You see, we don't go around preaching about ourselves. We preach that Jesus Christ is Lord, and we ourselves are your servants for Jesus' sake. For God, who said, "Let there be light in the darkness," has made this light shine in our hearts so we could know the glory of God that is seen in the face of Jesus Christ (2 Corinthians 4:1-6, New Living Translation).

God Has Given Us This Ministry

Paul gives us a bit of perspective right at the very beginning. The serving we do, as well as both the opportunity and the low hanging fruit person we serve, are all gifts from God. This is a critical foundation. None of what we do is *our* ministry. It all comes from, and belongs to, God. This is about ministering, serving, teaching and preaching God's way, not our own. We are serving on his behalf. We are fulfilling his purposes. We are putting his truth on display. We do all this for his glory.

We do well to remember that low hanging fruit people are not our targets. Rather they are people made in God's image, who he wants to redeem as his precious and beloved children. God will use those of us who already belong to him to reach those who are still lost.

We Do Not Lose Heart

Have you ever felt like you weren't making an impact for Jesus' kingdom? Have you ever become weary in the midst of serving? As Paul continues his thought, he speaks to the fatigue that so often accompanies our Christian witness and service.

Much of Christian service can be taxing: taxing physically because it's hard work, taxing mentally because it often involves real care and emotions, taxing spiritually because all service is in some way doing battle with the enemy. Remember, while we are working in partnership with the Holy Spirit to reach low hanging fruit people, we are at the same time working in opposition to Satan who desperately wants to keep them in the dark.

While Christian service — and seeing people come alive because of it — is personally fulfilling, we don't do it for our own benefit. Again, everything we do is for God's glory. Therefore, we do not lose heart. I know this on a personal level. In Chapter 4 I mentioned a very difficult season of life and ministry I had to endure — physically, I was recovering from two successive kidney surgeries; emotionally, I was a wreck dealing with depression and over two years of panic attacks and clinical anxiety; and spiritually, it was the darkest season of my life. More than once I thought of just giving up. And yet, that didn't happen.

This is not a book about anxiety and depression, but I want you to know that Paul's statement, "we never give up," (or as the New International Version puts it, "we do not lose heart") has real teeth. I don't do the things I do for my own benefit, but for God's glory. And it is amazing how he sustained me through that season. In fact, I have low hanging fruit stories of my own that came out of that season, as people with similar stories witnessed God's sustaining power in me. My point is simply this: serving can be excruciating, but some low hanging fruit people are best reached when they see God's faithfulness in our pain.

We Have Renounced Old Ways of Our Past

In order for us to be free to serve in the sacrificial way we are describing, Paul says, "We reject all shameful deeds and underhanded methods" in our relationships with other people. There is a tendency to think that Paul is talking here about our past way of life, but that's only part of his remark here. The grammar tells us that the shameful deeds (or what the NIV calls "secret ways") refers to our thoughts, not just our actions. Remember, the context here is losing heart. So Paul is talking about not giving in to our old ways of thinking. There were false apostles deceiving and misleading people in Corinth as Paul writes this letter. And it's possible that some of the Corinthians to whom he is writing have also been less than forthright in their relationships. None of this serves the mission of loving people.

Paul encourages us to resist what he calls "shameful desires" that may lead us to abandon the mission and ministry we have been given and take the easy way out. Our love is genuine and our message is completely truthful. When we say "yes" to Jesus, we say "yes" to becoming a servant just like him as well.

We Do Not Deceive or Distort

The truthfulness of our message and witness is foundational to loving like Jesus loves. We speak the truth in love just like our Jesus did. We lead with grace in all circumstances, but we never compromise the truth — just like our Jesus exemplified for us. We do not apologize for the requirements of our God, but we also are careful not to act in a way that adds insult to the corrective measures of God's Word. We are vessels of truth.

We speak the *plain* truth. I love this because Paul tells us that the conscience is the connection we have to them as low hanging fruit: "...and all who are honest know this" (v. 2). If the Holy Spirit is already preparing them — making them low hanging fruit people — their conscience will confirm what we say as truth! We speak the truth. We serve in love. We do not distort or "lessen" our demonstration of Jesus. We put the truth out there and let their conscience respond. And those who can't understand it are not ready yet (v. 3). Do you see it? We do not have to debate or argue with people who don't get it. We do not have to convince them — that's the Spirit's job. We just move on to those who the Holy Spirit has made ready.

It's important to note that there is a huge difference between those who respond with debate and those who respond with inquisitiveness. Both may ask tough questions, but only the latter is doing so because they truly want to understand. Low hanging fruit people will not be argumentative, but they may seem that way at first while they are feeling conviction and trying to figure things out. While we do not need to enter into debates with people who just want to argue, be patient and give low hanging fruit folks the attention they need. It's always exciting to witness real Spirit-led epiphanies as they happen. I once had a young man meet with me whose life was immersed in worldliness and addiction. But the Spirit was working on him. I watched with anticipation as, in a single conversation, he migrated from mild opposition to authentic interest, and then to some real conviction for his sinful lifestyle. We sat for over an hour and talked about a couple of relevant scripture passages that he had previously found frustrating but now felt were speaking directly to him (because they were!). He did not surrender to Christ in that first dialogue, but he moved really close and became very open to the work God was doing in his life. When I explained to him that I would be happy to be his pastor and give him wise counsel, but that my counsel and instruction would come from the Word of God, he actually said to me, "I would not expect you to do anything different." Too many such opportunities are missed for fear of opposition. We do not need to argue, but we do need to test their readiness for a truth conversation. If they resist, it's okay to wait for another time when they are more ready. But often they will open the door to a deeper conversation if we will be truly loving and forthright.

We Understand Our Enemy

Paul continues,

> *If the Good News we preach is hidden behind a veil, it is hidden only from people who are perishing. Satan, who is the god of this world, has blinded the minds of those who don't believe. They are unable to see the glorious light of the Good News. They don't understand this message about the glory of Christ, who is the exact likeness of God.* (2 Corinthians 4:3-4, New Living Translation)

The enemy, Satan, is the one who blinds the minds of people so they are unable to see the light of the gospel — and there is a lot of blindness around us today! We need to know our enemy. We do not need to fear him, for we belong to God as his precious, redeemed sons and daughters by the blood of Jesus. The Spirit of God in us is truly greater than he who is in this world (1 John 4:4). But we do need to understand the tactics Satan wields against people to keep them blind and in bondage.

> *First, Satan can masquerade as an "angel of light." Paul writes to the believers in Corinth about the false apostles who are deceiving*

many, "I am not surprised! Even Satan disguises himself as an angel of light. So it is no wonder that his servants also disguise themselves as servants of righteousness" (2 Corinthians 11:14-15, New Living Translation).

Satan deceives people into thinking his ways are right and good. He has been a deceiver from the beginning. Speaking to the Jews around him on one occasion, Jesus said,

"For you are the children of your father the devil, and you love to do the evil things he does. He was a murderer from the beginning. He has always hated the truth, because there is no truth in him. When he lies, it is consistent with his character; for he is a liar and the father of lies" (John 8:44, New Living Translation).

Second, Satan can orchestrate counterfeit miracles, signs and wonders. Speaking of the apocalyptic Man of Lawlessness who deceives many right before Jesus' glorious return, Paul says,

"This man will come to do the work of Satan with counterfeit power and signs and miracles. He will use every kind of evil deception to fool those on their way to destruction, because they refuse to love and accept the truth that would save them" (2 Thessalonians 2:9-10, New Living Translation).

It appears that those who are redeemed will not be deceived, but those who are not will not know the difference.

Third, Satan still tempts people just as he did in Eden. Writing to married believers about temptation, Paul warns,

"Do not deprive each other of sexual relations, unless you both agree to refrain from sexual intimacy for a limited time so you can give yourselves more completely to prayer. Afterward, you should come together again so that Satan won't be able to tempt you because of your lack of self-control" (1 Corinthians 7:5, New Living Translation).

Temptation is Satan's greatest tactic, and it even works against believers when they've stopped paying attention.

Fourth, Satan continuously schemes against us. He is especially masterful in undermining Christian unity by seeding unforgiveness among us. Paul writes,

> *"I wrote to you as I did to test you and see if you would fully comply with my instructions. When you forgive this man, I forgive him, too. And when I forgive whatever needs to be forgiven, I do so with Christ's authority for your benefit, so that Satan will not outsmart us. For we are familiar with his evil schemes"* (2 Corinthians 2:9-11, New Living Translation).

Our defense is understanding and daily applying the principles Paul teaches in the "armor of God." Paul writes to the Christians in Ephesus, "Put on all of God's armor so that you will be able to stand firm against all strategies of the devil" (Ephesians 6:11, New Living Translation).

Fifth, Satan sets traps for us. People who oppose the truth we are lovingly providing are particularly vulnerable. Paul writes to Timothy,

> *"Gently instruct those who oppose the truth. Perhaps God will change those people's hearts, and they will learn the truth. Then they will come to their senses and escape from the devil's trap. For they have been held captive by him to do whatever he wants"* (2 Timothy 2:25-26, New Living Translation).

Finally, Satan works *actively* against the gospel ministry. Paul writes to the Thessalonians,

> *"Dear brothers and sisters, after we were separated from you for a little while (though our hearts never left you), we tried very hard to come back because of our intense longing to see you again. We wanted very much to come to you, and I, Paul, tried again and again, but Satan prevented us"* (1 Thessalonians 2:17-18, New Living Translation).

Satan not only blinds the spiritual eyes of the unredeemed so they cannot understand and surrender to the gospel (2 Corinthians 4:4), he also works hard to put obstacles in the way of believers who purpose to reach them.

Again, we never need to fear Satan, but we do need to have a healthy grasp on his tactics. We have an enemy. There is very real opposition. That opposition may appear in human form, but we must always remember that someone is behind the scenes pulling the strings (Ephesians 6:12). Stay the course. We do not lose heart. Greater is our Jesus than the god of this age! This is never about our work or our success, but the ongoing work of the Holy Spirit. Our task is to rely upon him and continue looking for low hanging fruit.

It's All About Jesus

Paul concludes his instruction by reminding his readers that we all serve for Jesus' sake: "You see, we don't go around preaching about ourselves. We preach that Jesus Christ is Lord, and we ourselves are your servants for Jesus' sake" (2 Corinthians 4:5, New Living Translation). When we make it about ourselves, or about our goals, we are easily frustrated. But when we realize that we are *only* vessels in Jesus' hands, being used by him for *his* purposes, we can remain open and available for him to shine his gospel light through our lives. When low hanging fruit people encounter us, they are actually encountering the Lord of Glory himself!

Paul says that God has made his light to shine in us. We do well to remember that we are not the light, Jesus is. The Apostle John calls Jesus the light (John 1:1-9). When we are redeemed and filled with the Holy Spirit, we are vessels of that light. In fact, Jesus himself calls us the light of the world for this very reason.

> *"You are the light of the world—like a city on a hilltop that cannot be hidden. No one lights a lamp and then puts it under a basket. Instead, a lamp is placed on a stand, where it gives light to everyone in the house. In the same way, let your good deeds shine out for all to see, so that everyone will praise your heavenly Father" (Matthew 5:14-16, New Living Translation).*

As we serve in this way — lovingly but unapologetically speaking the truth and addressing the needs of the low hanging fruit people God brings into our lives — we become gospel lights shining very brightly in this dark world. Those who are already prepared by the Holy Spirit will "see the light" and will come to it. It's not us, but the light of Jesus in us that makes the difference.

Practical Application

Friend, if you are a follower of Jesus Christ, what we are describing is your life. We are not redeemed merely for our own salvation, but so that humanity's original purpose is fully and completely restored in us: to be like God and to represent him throughout all creation. We are redeemed to become instruments used by the Holy Spirit for the redemption of others. When we say "yes" to Jesus and leave our old ways behind, this becomes our life. It doesn't necessarily mean we have to change careers, although for some it might. But it does mean that in every area of life — family, friends, career, hobbies, leisure, *everything* — we are an intentional light to the world for Jesus.

Everything about our lives with other people is now about our witness. The way we live our life is always about how we bring Jesus to those around us. We always have our testimony in mind — finding ways to introduce the love, grace and truth of Jesus to people. Not everyone will understand, because the Holy Spirit is still working on some people! But every day someone will see the light of Jesus because of you. They will see Jesus *in* you — in the way you love, in the way you speak to them, in the way you serve them, in the truth you show them both verbally and by your lifestyle.

You might be thinking, "Yes, but won't some take advantage of me when I do this?" The answer is yes. Some definitely will. That is not your concern — it is Jesus'. While we are called by God to be good stewards of the time and resources he gives us, we are not to withdraw. The same Bible that tells us the early church shared with everyone who had need, also tells us that those who will not work will not eat (2 Thessalonians 3:10). Here's the bottom line: our time and resources are not our own, they are God's. And God will hold both the giver and the receiver accountable. Taking advantage of the love and service of God's people is wicked, yes (especially if one takes them away from those who really need them). But God only expects us to be good stewards and *use* what he gives us (Matthew 25:14-30). He is the one who will deal with such wickedness. It is our job to remain faithful to the task we have been given. We love and serve low hanging fruit people, leaving judgement up to him.

CHAPTER 8
Evangelizing People

"Listen, O Israel! The Lord is our God, the Lord alone. And you must love the Lord your God with all your heart, all your soul, and all your strength. And you must commit yourselves wholeheartedly to these commands that I am giving you today. Repeat them again and again to your children. Talk about them when you are at home and when you are on the road, when you are going to bed and when you are getting up. Tie them to your hands and wear them on your forehead as reminders. Write them on the doorposts of your house and on your gates"
(Deuteronomy 6:4-9, New Living Translation).

At some point in your relationship with your low hanging fruit friends, you'll have the opportunity to explain to them what Jesus has done for us all. While it's crucial to remember that we never really bring people to the point of conversion — that's the Holy Spirit's job (John 16:8) — we do have an important role to play in that partnership. Sharing the gospel is not just telling them about salvation, but is also *showing* them what a redeemed life looks like.

In Chapter 6 I referred to a tool developed by Jim Engle called *The Engle Scale of Evangelism*,[13] which shows the vital relationship between disciple making and evangelism. Evangelism is not simply an event that leads to conversion, but part of a spiritual journey on which you walk with someone to full maturity in Christ. Biblically, evangelism is integrated into the overall activity of disciple making. In his 1974 address at the World Congress on International Evangelization in Lausanne, Switzerland, theologian John R.W. Stott explains that evangelism is not necessarily "winning" people to Christ, but simply announcing to them the good news of the gospel whether they accept it or not. Evangelism is that part of disciple making where we lovingly nudge people toward conversion, but we don't stop there. The spiritual formation work continues until we (or someone else) help them reach spiritual maturity and Christlike character. The people we've been calling low hanging fruit are those whom the Holy Spirit has prepared to move forward along that journey.

God's Original Instructions

It's important to understand evangelism as part of God's original instructions to his people. God has always wanted a relationship with human beings. Always. When humanity rejected God's rule and reign in the Garden of Eden, he immediately began working toward restoring that relationship. Deuteronomy 6:4-9 is a significant part of that restoration plan. It's called the *Shema* and is really a creedal statement for the Hebrew people, declaring that God is *one*. But God's instruction through Moses didn't stop there. He goes on to talk about how this covenant relationship with God is passed down from one generation to the next. And the process he gives outlines precisely how we do evangelism today.

The Beginning: Our Authentic Love for God

Teaching is easy. You can take someone to a textbook and teach them facts you haven't already known yourself. But it is impossible to *impart* something that is not already real and present in your life. The old adage is true: when it comes to the Christian Faith, more is caught than taught. Nowhere is this more critical than in helping the next spiritual generation

---

13 James F. Engle and Wilbert Norton, *What's Gone Wrong with the Harvest: A Communication Strategy for the Church and World Evangelism*, Grand Rapids: Zondervan Publishing House, 1975.

to fall in love with our Heavenly Father. If all we show people is our academic knowledge of God — our theology — and not our love relationship with him, we have failed. Please understand: *all* evangelism and disciple making begins with our own love relationship with God. Notice that Moses expresses this point in what Jesus will later call "The Greatest Commandment."

> *"Listen, O Israel! The LORD is our God, the LORD alone. And you must love the LORD your God with all your heart, all your soul, and all your strength"* (Deuteronomy 6:4-5, New Living Translation).

> *"But when the Pharisees heard that he had silenced the Sadducees with his reply, they met together to question him again. One of them, an expert in religious law, tried to trap him with this question: 'Teacher, which is the most important commandment in the law of Moses?'*
>
> *Jesus replied, " 'You must love the LORD your God with all your heart, all your soul, and all your mind.' This is the first and greatest commandment. A second is equally important: 'Love your neighbor as yourself.' The entire law and all the demands of the prophets are based on these two commandments"* (Matthew 22:37-40, New Living Translation).

Here is a critical truth: you cannot truly evangelize low hanging fruit people if you do not first have a real and all-encompassing love of God yourself. We have already talked about the importance of authentic love when it comes to serving. The source of that love for everyone around us is our own love relationship with God. This love must be evident.

Obedience on Display

Love and obedience go hand in hand. Jesus makes this clear to his disciples:

> *"Those who accept my commandments and obey them are the ones who love me. And because they love me, my Father will love them. And I will love them and reveal myself to each of them"* (John 14:21, New Living Translation).

He goes on to explain,

> *"I have loved you even as the Father has loved me. Remain in my love. When you obey my commandments, you remain in my love, just as I obey my Father's commandments and remain in his love"* (John 15:9-10, New Living Translation).

Because evangelism and disciple making are so inseparably tied together, leading low hanging fruit people toward faith in Christ is much more about displaying our own faith relationship than simply telling them a message of salvation! Moses instructs,

> *"...you must commit yourselves wholeheartedly to these commands that I am giving you today"* (Deuteronomy 6:6, New Living Translation).

Again the example of a loving and faithful relationship with God is the key. When the next spiritual generation sees it and experiences it in your life, they are much more likely to desire it in their own. People all around us have every right to call us hypocrites when our lives do not display the relationship with God we are proclaiming to them.

Impress Them On The Next Generation

When we love God with our whole being (Deuteronomy 6:5) and consistently display our own faithful obedience to him for all to see (Deuteronomy 6:6) we can then effectively galvanize real faith in our children and others. The word "impress" here is actually the Hebrew word "to whet" or "to sharpen" as in a knife or a sword! We are to take the commands of God — which will ultimately lead the way of salvation in Christ one day — and sharpen or shape our literal and spiritual children with them! Low hanging fruit people have been made ready by the Holy Spirit to receive that investment. Think about it: as we put our love and obedience on display and then talk about the commands and instructions of God (that we are clearly striving to live by ourselves), we are actually used by the Holy Spirit to shape people! Each opportunity we have to *demonstrate* the gospel to people shapes them. They may not realize it at first, but the Holy Spirit is at work!

This work is to be a consistent part of our home life. Moses commands,

> *"Repeat [these commands] again and again to your children. Talk about them when you are at home and when you are on the road, when you are going to bed and when you are getting up. Tie them to your hands and wear them on your forehead as reminders. Write them on the doorposts of your house and on your gates"* (Deuteronomy 6:7-9, New Living Translation).

Of course the immediate context here is family, but this same process should also be applied for anyone who is invited into our homes. We need to ask:

When someone comes into my home, particularly those made ready by the Holy Spirit, are they enveloped with the Good News?

1. Is my home a place of real peace?
2. Is our home life a clear reflection of a redeemed life in Christ?
3. Is my life at home an honest reflection of my love for God?
4. Do people see me as faithful and obedient to God in my home as they do at church?

Not only do we live out the commands and instructions of God in our homes, but also as we live life out in the world around us. "When you are on the road..." is a reference to our regular daily life. As we're moving through our days from place to place, engaging low hanging fruit people, we need to ask:

1. Do those who know me see someone who lives a life of love and peace?
2. Does my lifestyle reflect Jesus' redemption?
3. Do I treat the people I meet each day as those who are deeply loved by our Heavenly Father?

4. Does my day to day life lure people to ask me about my "better way of living"?

Love and Obedience All Day, Everywhere

We cannot export to others what is not real and consistent in our own private lives. We are to make love and obedience our last thought in the evening. "When we lay down...", our last thoughts of the day before we sleep should be of our wonderful God. And as we nudge people closer to a mature relationship with God in Jesus Christ, we show them how to do this for themselves. Each night, we meditate on God's love for us and recount how we've demonstrated that love back to him and to others. We meditate on how our life in Christ (our witness) went that day. We meditate on what we've learned from God's Word during the day. We meditate on what we've seen God do that day. We meditate on the people God has allowed us to influence that day. We meditate on the salvation that is ours in Christ, setting our mind at peace and preparing us to rest in real joy and fulfillment. Finally, we stop and pray for all those God has brought us to influence for Jesus, that the investments we have made in partnership with the Holy Spirit will bear fruit.

We are to make love and obedience our first thought in the morning. Just like our evening routine, we have a morning routine to set us up for the day. *"When we are getting up..."* we begin with gratitude for our relationship with God in Christ and for the forgiveness and salvation he has given us. We express our own love to him in prayer and even in praise and worship (I have found worship choruses using a music app on my phone are very helpful here). We set aside time in the morning to spend with God's Word — this both settles our minds and hearts for the day, and also gives the Holy Spirit an opportunity to give us our daily "marching orders." We lovingly ask God what he has for us that day — and we ask him to help us so that we don't miss any divine appointments he has for us. We express our desire to love him fully. We express our desire to be faithful. We express our desire to remain obedient and ask for his help in these. From there we make the glorious life we share in Christ the foundation of every discussion in some way.

Practical Helps for the Task

The Israelites had tools that were designed to keep them "in tune" with God throughout the day. They had little boxes with the scroll of the Law called phylacteries as a means of carrying God's Word with them on their person. We don't use such reminders today, but we have lots of tools that can accomplish the same purpose. We can set up reminders on our phones to stop and pray or read scripture at different times during the day. We can practice scripture memorization (more on that in the next chapter). I have one friend that writes out a daily verse or a word from the Lord during devotions on a 3x5 card and carries it with him. He reviews and prayerfully meditates on that message all day long. I have another friend that does something similar with Post-it Notes — placing them strategically where they will be seen (on the side of the computer monitor, the bathroom mirror, the car dashboard, etc.) so she encounters God's Word during the day. Be creative. And be sure to include others in what you do as well.

We are to place reminders around the home as well. Christian artwork is not just decor — it can be instructive. Stained glass windows in the cathedrals of old served a similar purpose: they taught people the story of the Bible. What do we put before our eyes during the day? What scripture reminders have we placed about the house? What books are we reading? What television shows are we watching? And what distractions are in our home that actually move us further away from God, his Word and the gospel?

Again, we cannot invest in others — low hanging fruit people or anyone else — what we do not already have hidden in our hearts. We cannot effectively evangelize our low hanging fruit friends if we are not already living the life to which we are wooing them. We don't do these things to be legalistic, but to be faithful. When we truly love God with everything we are, when we put our own obedience on display and as we grow in our understanding of God's Word and apply it in our own lives first before impressing it on others, our witness is strong and has credibility. This is the kind of witness in partnership with the Holy Spirit that draws people to Christ where they are converted and start their own journey to Christian maturity.

Presenting the Basics

Let me conclude this chapter with just a very brief overview of the gospel basics for those who may not yet have ever shared their faith. Let me emphasize that it is not *what* you know but *who* you know here that makes the difference. If the Holy Spirit has primed your low hanging fruit friend to hear and receive the good news Jesus is offering them, he will use you in this effort no matter how "green" you might be.

If sharing the gospel is from the life and fruit of Jesus already evident in you, especially when it is done in the context of a redemptive relationship like we've been describing in this book, then your low hanging fruit friend will undoubtedly receive your witness as part of the trust and love they already have with you. And if that redemptive relationship has been developing for some time, it is likely many of the things I share here have already been established. Use the following as a guide, not a "punch list" to pursue legalistically. Remember, anything you might miss here is still under the supervision of the Holy Spirit. There will always be other opportunities to add important doctrinal truths at a later time. Millions of little children have genuinely come to saving faith in Christ without understanding all the doctrines of soteriology (what the bible teaches about salvation) and have learned what they needed over time as they matured. It's near impossible to mess this up. Besides, success is not up to you – it's up to the Spirit. Take a deep breath and step out in faith.

So just how does one share the gospel of Jesus Christ? There are many valid methods and approaches, but in my opinion, there are four major components:

1. *Share God's Heart for Humanity* - Tell them about God's love and original intent for all humanity (refer back to Chapter 1). Let them know God created us as objects of his infinite love and his desire was to share his rule and reign over creation with us. Tell them God's desire has never changed.

2. *Share Humanity's Rebellion and Its Impact on All Generations* - Explain what happened as the first humans surrendered themselves to the deceiver, Satan. Explain that

the whole Bible is the story of God working to redeem us. He's wanted us to experience forgiveness and restoration with him all along.

3. *Share God's Ultimate Remedy for Our Sin* - Tell them just a little about how God worked to rebuild humanity's relationship with him. He did this through covenants. Like the Covenant of Christian Marriage is the life-long relationship between a husband and wife, so God instituted what were to be lasting covenants with his people (Aside: Did you know God made his covenant with his people five different times in the Old Testament? He made it with Adam [original], with Noah, with Abraham, with Moses, and with David). God's people kept breaking these covenants. So God ultimately established the New Covenant with all of us through Jesus Christ. Jesus died on the cross to pay the penalty for humanity's ongoing sin problem and create a brand new forever relationship with God on our behalf.

4. *Share Our Needed Response - Faith* - No gift ever becomes ours until we receive it. So it is with our forgiveness, salvation and restoration with God. Humanity turned their backs on God in the Garden of Eden when they surrendered to the deceiver, Satan. So now, we must turn our backs on Satan today and surrender to Jesus as our Savior and King. We do not fully receive the incredible gift he has given us until we surrender to him and enter afresh into a loving relationship with him.

There are lots of different methods and tools out there from pastors, churches, evangelists and other ministries that are helpful. But if you cover the four things above so they are understood and accepted, you've done your part. The rest is up to the Holy Spirit (John 16:5-11). That said, here are some suggestions if you'd like to add to your evangelism toolbelt.

- *The Wordless Book* (Child Evangelism Fellowship - www.cefonline.com)
- *Two Diagnostic Questions* (Evangelism Explosion - www.evangelismexplosion.org - there is a whole course on their method if you're interested)
- *The Four Spiritual Laws* (CRU - www.cru.org)
- *Steps to Peace with God* (Billy Graham Evangelistic Association - www.billygraham.org)
- *One Verse Evangelism* (The Navigators - www.navigators.org - this is one of the simplest presentations I know and I've used it to lead many children to Christ)
- *Knowing God Personally* (Sonlife - www.sonlife.com)
- *Three Circles* (North American Mission Board - www.namb.net)
- *The Romans Road* (an old faithful process used for years employing seven verses from the Book of Romans to lay out the gospel - you can easily find it online)

There are many more tools and methods, but these are some of the most popular. Ultimately, however, you don't want to depend on a tool because your explanation of the gospel might become "canned" and less impactful. The best way to share Christ is directly from your own heart and experience. And I guarantee you that your low hanging fruit friends will respond more to that in the context of a redemptive relationship than to anything else.

CHAPTER 9
Memorizing Scripture Together

How can a young person stay pure? By obeying your word.
I have tried hard to find you—
don't let me wander from your commands.
I have hidden your word in my heart, that I might not sin against you.
I praise you, O LORD; teach me your decrees.
I have recited aloud all the regulations you have given us.
I have rejoiced in your laws as much as in riches.
I will study your commandments and reflect on your ways.
I will delight in your decrees and not forget your word.
Be good to your servant, that I may live and obey your word.
Open my eyes to see the wonderful truths in your instructions.
(Psalm 119:9-18, New Living Translation)

The struggle is real. It does not matter how genuinely each of us may desire to live our lives in a way that truly honors Jesus Christ, we will slip. Oh how many Christians would like to live a God-focused life — one that woos people toward Jesus — but cannot seem to find success! Our thoughts wander and betray us. Our hearts expose the sinful content within. We say and do things that hurt people and tarnish our witness. How do we work on this problem? In truth, *we* don't. It's the work of the Holy Spirit — but there are ways in which we can partner with his efforts, growing in personal righteousness in the process. Our loving Heavenly Father gives us great guidance in Psalm 119. The Word of God itself has a powerful impact, but we must engage it for this to happen. And, as you can imagine, that impact is not only personal but also upon our low hanging fruit relationships. In fact, for our purposes in this chapter, I will discuss how to spend time in the scriptures *together* — for deeper fellowship, for understanding and to align our hearts more perfectly with Jesus.

The Longest Psalm

Psalm 119 is not only the longest psalm in the Book of Psalms, but the single longest chapter in the entire bible. While no author is listed, most scholars believe that the collection comes from King David. The author is clearly someone who knew the sting of enemy pursuit and its related suffering. The collection of songs centers on themes of righteousness, faithfulness and purity, all the result of a vibrant love, study and memorization of God's Word — his law and statutes.

A Key Question and Its Answer

The psalmist asks a key question and then gives us the answer:

> *"How can a young person stay pure?*
> *By obeying your word"* (Psalm 119:9, New Living Translation).

We live according to the Word of God. It is given to us as life's "owners manual," written by the One who created us and all life. His instructions are true. His instructions are best. And there are few ways to learn to live according to the Word of God better than to memorize it. But it's hard to find people in today's church who regularly and consistently practice this critical discipline. In fact, most would likely admit they don't even know where to start. Just how does one begin committing scripture to memory? How do we do this for personal blessings? And, in keeping with our current topic, how do we do this with and for those we are wooing toward Jesus?

Guidance from the Psalmist

David actually gives us guidance on committing God's Word to heart. His instruction is a great place to start as we connect with others in this common quest – and he outlines it in the psalm itself.

1. *We begin with intentionality (Psalm 119:10).* This is a significant first step because it's our primary part in the process. We seek God with all our heart. Remember our discussion of the *Shema* in Chapter 8 – the creed of the Israelites and what Jesus called The Greatest Commandment. Based upon our redeemed love relationship with God, we seek him with every fiber of our being. We love him with all our heart, all our soul, all our mind, and all our strength. We pursue him body, soul and spirit. To do this, we must act *on purpose.* It can become more natural over time as we mature in our walk with Christ, but it begins with rabid intentionality.

2. *We ask God for his help (Psalm 119:10).* Thankfully, we do not attempt this process on our own. Notice that we have a partner! We do our part, but God picks up the slack! Along with David, "...don't let me wander from your commands" must be our ongoing prayer! It is the combination of our own purposeful pursuit of God and God's work in us by the Holy Spirit that gives us success. Honestly, we cannot do this successfully on our own – at least not expecting to bear any fruit.

3. *We memorize scripture for a reason (Psalm 119:11).* David proclaims, *"I have hidden your word in my heart, that I might not sin against you."* We memorize scripture because it can become the primary tool the Holy Spirit can use to guide us away from sin and selfishness! The Word of God defines sin for us. The Word of God explains the escape from sin. The Word of God imparts to us a deep, personal understanding of God's character.

4. *We praise and surrender afresh (Psalm 119:12).* We cannot come to this process begrudgingly. We absolutely cannot do it out of duty. We must genuinely want it. We must surrender to it – to the work of the Holy Spirit in us. We must come to

a place where we delight in it (we'll talk more about this in a minute). Being in the Word of God should stir praise in us. It may not at the beginning – especially if it seems foreign. But if we remain intentional and in willing partnership with the Holy Spirit, over time it will indeed become that. David sings, *"I praise you, O LORD; teach me your decrees."* The combination of praise and an openness to be taught is powerful indeed!

5. *We speak what we're learning out loud (Psalm 119:13).* Scripture memorization is best done *out loud* – and also with other people when possible. This is one of the reasons memorizing God's Word with others is so helpful. We should speak it to ourselves when we're alone. We should speak it to others when possible. We should incorporate it into our dialog as appropriate with people we meet each day – yes, even strangers! This may seem odd to us at first because it is so counter-cultural, but do not shy away from this! As we exercise the Word of God we're hiding in our hearts, it will quickly begin to impact others. And there is an added benefit: we'll begin to identify more low hanging fruit people as we do!

6. *We rejoice in the fruit and change it brings (Psalm 119:14).* As we learn the scripture, it will begin its work in us. We should return praise to God for what he is doing in us through his Word. We should praise him when we're alone. We should praise him for it as a testimony in worship with others. David tells us of this transformation's value, *"I have rejoiced in your laws as much as in riches."*

7. *We grow in our understanding of its value (Psalm 119:14).* As the scriptures embed themselves in our hearts, they transform everything about us over time – our worldview, our beliefs, what's important to us and our behavior. Worldly people are consumed with wealth and stuff; however, this is just a distraction in the plot of the enemy of our souls. The greatest value we can realize in this life is to become more and more like our Jesus.

8. *We "chew" on what we're learning all day long (Psalm 119:15).* David sings, *"I will study your commandments..."* This phrase in Hebrew has the sense of deep meditation – not just a quick perusal, but a dwelling on a particular topic for complete understanding. We find ways to keep the passage we're studying before us throughout the whole day.

9. *We consider what it requires of us and we adjust (Psalm 119:15).* David continues, *"...and reflect on your ways."* Reflection here is also an interesting term. It actually means, "I will fix my eyes upon," or "I will look and consider." We keep ourselves affixed to the Word and allow it to transform us.

10. *We delight in living out the Word of God (Psalm 119:16).* It takes time, but the goal is to get to the place where we actually take beautiful pleasure in the scripture and the impact it is having (uncomfortable and challenging as it may sometimes be) on our lives. I promise you, it will indeed happen if you persevere. My whole life and career as a pastor are staked on this! When you see the impact it makes on you from the inside out, and the fruit it bears through you in the lives of other people, you'll be delighted too!

Addressing a Common Problem

Many people struggle to establish a consistent daily "quiet time" where they spend time in both prayer and in reading the scriptures. I would remind you that we have an enemy who is deeply invested in keeping humanity from any kind of relationship with God. He works hard to prevent people from ever coming to Christ (2 Corinthians 4:4). And you can bet that, once someone slips through his grasp, he will stop at nothing to obstruct them in every effort to grow in Christlikeness.

Beyond the spiritual opposition we face, let me make a suggestion to simplify the process for you that may seem counter-intuitive. Don't use a devotional guide. I have no problem with good devotional guides of all kinds – in fact I use one myself. But when one begins the journey of Scripture memorization, I've found it's best to stick just to the scriptures themselves. Sometimes the very systems we employ to help us be more consistent actually get in the way of our consistency. And, to be honest, the Word of God itself has great power (2 Timothy 3:16-17).

When you begin committing scripture to your heart – and especially if you are doing this with a low hanging fruit partner – just stick to the Bible. It's okay to use a Bible reading plan of some kind (there are many available online), but just let the scripture do its work. The prophet Isaiah announces,

> *"My thoughts are nothing like your thoughts," says the Lord.*
> *"And my ways are far beyond anything you could imagine.*
> *For just as the heavens are higher than the earth,*
> *so my ways are higher than your ways*
> *and my thoughts higher than your thoughts.*
> *"The rain and snow come down from the heavens*
> *and stay on the ground to water the earth.*
> *They cause the grain to grow,*
> *producing seed for the farmer*
> *and bread for the hungry.*
> ***It is the same with my word.***
> ***I send it out, and it always produces fruit.***
> ***It will accomplish all I want it to,***
> ***and it will prosper everywhere I send it.***
> *You will live in joy and peace.*
> *The mountains and hills will burst into song,*
> *and the trees of the field will clap their hands!*
> *Where once there were thorns, cypress trees will grow.*
> *Where nettles grew, myrtles will sprout up.*
> *These events will bring great honor to the Lord's name;*
> *they will be an everlasting sign of his power and love"*
> (Isaiah 55:8-13, New Living Translation, **emphasis mine**).

God tells us through the prophet that his Word will accomplish its purpose (v. 11), but also notice the results – joy, peace, fruitful labors, honoring the Lord and experiencing his power and love!

A Transformational Idea

In his book, *Ordinary Hero: Becoming a Disciple Who Makes a Difference*[14], Neil Cole gives a suggestion that I have found incredibly fruitful over the years – what he calls "Life Transformation Groups" or "LTGs." Cole writes, "LTGs are a simple, yet powerful, way to reproduce disciples." I agree – and they are awesome for scripture memorization partnerships with low hanging fruit folks.

LTGs build community and are truly non-threatening. They are made up of two or three people (any more, and you divide into new groups). They are gender-specific (meaning men meet with men and women meet with women). There is no need for a leader, and they really only have three tasks to complete together on a weekly basis:

1. Sin is confessed to one another for mutual accountability

2. Scripture is read repetitively, in entire context, and in community

3. Souls are prayed for strategically, specifically, and continuously

These groups are powerful for many reasons, but when it comes to that second task, this is where scripture memorization can really take hold. If the duo or triad are reading and meditating on a passage together, they can also agree together to memorize a portion of it (you might only do single verses at first). They can recite the memorized portion together as they gather. They can check in with each other during the rest of the week and rehearse the passage together over the phone. And they can hold each other accountable to have the verse committed to memory by the next

---

14   Cole, Neil, *Ordinary Hero: Becoming a Disciple Who Makes a Difference*, (Grand Rapids, MI: Baker Books, 2011).

gathering. I've seen this work with many folks. You might give LTGs a try – you'll see a large number of benefits in your relationship with low hanging fruit people.

A Practical Process

When it comes to the actual task of committing a passage of scripture to memory, there are all kinds of processes out there. In the end, use one that works best for you and your low hanging fruit friend. But I must admit that, on this point, I was actually inspired by my daughter, Lauren. She and her friends have memorized scripture together since college. And I have found that the process she uses is one of the easiest and more effective ones I've learned. I'll end this chapter with what she has taught me.

1. *Choose a portion of scripture.* This method works for big and small portions alike, but again, if you're new to this, begin small and work your way up.

2. *Letters and punctuation.* On a piece of paper, write down the first letters of each word in your chosen passage with the correct capitalization and punctuation.

3. *Read.* Read the portion of scripture several times from your Bible. Do this slowly and meditatively. Let it soak into your heart and mind.

4. *Back to your letters.* Go and look at your "letter notes" and see how much of your selected passage you can recite just from looking at the letters and punctuation. Don't be discouraged as this process takes time, but keep at it.

5. *Alternate.* Alternate back and forth between your actual bible and your "letter notes," trying to increase how much of your selected passage you can do only from the notes. Do this until you can recite your whole passage only from the letters.

6. *Post it.* Put copies of your "letter notes" in places where you'll see them throughout the day, and practice every time

they remind you. Lauren told me that she and her roommates would put a copy in a ziplock bag and even post them in the shower. Be creative. Be consistent.

7. *Block some out.* As you get more familiar with your passage, begin blocking out (or erasing) sections of letters where you already have confidence. Do this until you can recite the whole thing completely without the help of your "letter notes."

Lauren and her friends have memorized large portions of God's Word using this method. They were able to commit the Book of James and portions of Paul's letter to the Philippians to heart and still remember it now many years later.

Again, the above is only one possible method, but I know it has helped many people memorize a lot of scripture. In the end, you and your low hanging fruit partner will have to find the method that works best for you. But do it! You, like David, will discover how wonderful are the benefits of hiding God's Word in your heart.

CHAPTER 10
Real Fellowship

All the believers devoted themselves to the apostles' teaching, and to fellowship, and to sharing in meals (including the Lord's Supper), and to prayer.

A deep sense of awe came over them all, and the apostles performed many miraculous signs and wonders. And all the believers met together in one place and shared everything they had. They sold their property and possessions and shared the money with those in need. They worshiped together at the Temple each day, met in homes for the Lord's Supper, and shared their meals with great joy and generosity—all the while praising God and enjoying the goodwill of all the people. And each day the Lord added to their fellowship those who were being saved.
(Acts 2:42-47, New Living Translation)

We're one of those families that can quote the entire script of certain movies. I think every single one of us could recite *The Princess Bride* from memory. And it's probably the same with both trilogies of *The Lord of the Rings* and *The Hobbit.* My wife and I have the special extended boxed sets of both. The joke in our home at bedtime is that "we'll just watch ten minutes" and then go to bed. Never happens.

In the first *LOTR* movie, Hobbits Frodo and Sam find themselves among a mixed group they never dreamed they'd even meet, let alone to be a part. Once the ring is determined by Gandalf to be the One Ring (you'll have to see the movie, but this is an ominous thing that sets the stage for the whole trilogy), Elrond the Elf King calls a council of Wizards, Elves, Dwarves and Men (and the Hobbits) to decide what must be done. J.R.R. Tolkien was masterful in writing this part. All the drama and brokenness of the relationships between these beings comes to light in less than 5 minutes. And it is the little Hobbit, Frodo, who must take responsibility. Elrond calls from among the others those who will help and protect Frodo on this quest: Gandalf the Wizard, Boromir and Aragorn from the leaders of men, Gimli from the dwarves, and Legolas from the elves join Frodo, Sam, Merry and Pippin the Hobbits. Together, they must help Frodo destroy the One Ring. Elrond is pleased with this conclusion and proclaims, "Nine companions. So be it. You shall be the Fellowship of the Ring."

Fellowship. It's one of the most misunderstood concepts in today's church. It really has very little to do with Sunday attendance or gatherings or "eatin' meetin's." I know the word is actually synonymous with fried chicken in some circles – but this completely misses the point of the term. Fellowship is "relationship with a reason." Fellowship is gathering for the purposes of fulfilling a mission. This is why Elrond's proclamation is so poignant. The nine companions are companions on a common mission. And they must work together, care for each other and protect each other so that the mission can succeed. So it is with the church.

Fellowship in the Church

Many, including myself, understand Acts 2:42-47 (above) to be the ideal description of Jesus' church. In other words, this is the way it's *supposed* to be. Back in Chapter 1, we discussed how the early church, as described in Acts 2:42-47, was a place where Peter and John were able to mature and prepare for their respective parts in Jesus' mission. Of particular importance is Acts 2:42. You can go back and read the details in Chapter 1, but for our purposes here, let me quickly summarize:

1. *They were devoted to apostolic teaching.* All of the followers of Jesus collectively listened to, learned from and applied the

teaching of those who were direct students of Jesus. Jesus discipled them, and they in turn discipled the next spiritual generation of the newly birthed church.

2. *They were devoted to the fellowship.* As we noted in Chapter 1, there is a definite article in front of the Greek word for fellowship. All the followers of Jesus were devoted to *the* fellowship of believers. Like Elrond's Fellowship of the Ring, the newly birthed church was a growing gathering of people on a common mission together.

3. *They were devoted to the sharing of meals.* All of the followers of Jesus were not only consistent in celebrating what we now call The Lord's Table (communion), but they actually ate meals with each other regularly. For the newly birthed church, which was made up at this time predominantly of Jews, there was nothing that demonstrated their intimacy with each other more than eating in each others' homes.

4. *They were devoted to prayer.* All of the followers of Jesus were knowledgeable and persistent in all aspects of prayer: conversations with God, urgent pleas, intercession for the will of God in people's lives, and thanksgiving (1 Timothy 2:1). The newly birthed church had great power and saw many miraculous things because of their devotion to prayer.

Fellowship among Christians is not just about affinity. It is not just an activity in which we participate for fun, meals and mutual edification. These things can certainly happen, but biblically, fellowship is really about the mission. Anyone who has ever participated in a short term missions team in another culture knows this. Team members who, perhaps, never met each other before the mission trip become like family before it's over. Often, relationships established on the mission last a lifetime. Members of the military have a similar experience.

As we begin to understand this important nuance about the biblical idea of fellowship, then we also realize that Luke (the author of Acts) was very intentional in his choice of verbiage when describing life in that early church. Did you notice he said that the believers were *devoted* to those critical components of church life? He did not say *committed*. Devotion and commitment may appear to be the same – and in fact, they are used as synonyms in some dictionaries. But there is a very important difference between these terms. Commitment is with the head. It is adherence to an agenda, platform, concept, strategy or idea. Devotion, on the other hand, is with the heart. Devotion is a form of love. These terms may have very similar usage, but they are not the same. As we now go into more detail describing biblical fellowship and what it means for our low hanging fruit colleagues, we must realize that it all begins with authentic devotion.

Fellowship Demonstrates a Common Sense of God's Presence

"A deep sense of awe came over them all..."
(Acts 2:43, New Living Translation)

Everyone in this new, fledgling church community was filled with the awe and wonder of God. These people are in relationship with each other, and also with God. The apostles – those who had been disciples of Jesus – were still present and the growth of the movement is nothing short of miraculous. God's presence by the Holy Spirit is evident every single day. Imagine gathering for worship and there is a clear God-encounter every single time! In this kind of fellowship, that is to be the norm. Low hanging fruit people will begin to experience real reverence, awe and adoration of God when they are invited into a community like this.

Unfortunately today many congregations just gather and go through their religious motions, rituals and recitations. They enjoy each other's company, but their fellowship is about their affinity, not Christ's mission. They pray, but few actually see answers to their prayers. They serve, but it rarely has a clear gospel witness attached. And in still other cases, congregations have departed from the foundations of the gospel all together. About them Paul writes to young Timothy,

> *You should know this, Timothy, that in the last days there will be very difficult times. For people will love only themselves and their money. They will be boastful and proud, scoffing at God, disobedient to their parents, and ungrateful. They will consider nothing sacred. They will be unloving and unforgiving; they will slander others and have no self-control. They will be cruel and hate what is good. They will betray their friends, be reckless, be puffed up*

with pride, and love pleasure rather than God. They will act religious, but they will reject the power that could make them godly. Stay away from people like that! (2 Timothy 3:1-5, New Living Translation).

What an incredible statement: *"They will act religious, but they will reject the power that could make them godly."* A community that does not regularly and consistently have a common sense of God's presence is not the kind of fellowship we are describing.

Fellowship Demonstrates Kingdom Authority

"...and the apostles performed many miraculous signs and wonders" (Acts 2:43)

You may have gathered already from what I have written that I am not theologically what is called a "Cessationist." Cessationists believe that the more spectacular signs and wonders described in the New Testament departed after the formal completion of the canon of Scripture. Many of my dearest colleagues in ministry and in my own denomination would believe this. I respectfully do not. While I share most of their concerns about excesses and some truly unbiblical demonstrations of "wonders" in the name of the Holy Spirit, I believe such things are counterfeits but that the real thing is still very much present in Christ's church today.

We must always guard against counterfeits. The early church did as well. In fact, Jesus himself warned us about such things:

> *"Then if anyone tells you, 'Look, here is the Messiah,' or 'There he is,' don't believe it. For false messiahs and false prophets will rise up and perform great signs and wonders so as to deceive, if possible, even God's chosen ones. See, I have warned you about this ahead of time" (Matthew 24:23-25, New Living Translation).*

And Paul writes to the Christians in Thessalonica,

> *"Then the man of lawlessness will be revealed, but the Lord Jesus will slay him with the breath of his mouth and destroy him by the splendor of his coming.*

> *This man will come to do the work of Satan with counterfeit power and signs and miracles. He will use every kind of evil deception to fool those on their way to destruction, because they refuse to love and accept the truth that would save them"* (2 Thessalonians 2:8-10, New Living Translation).

The fact that we are warned about counterfeits means that the real thing exists. Years ago I worked in the vault of a national bank. I was trained by the FBI how to recognize counterfeit bills. You know how they trained us? By helping us know the real thing so well that literally *any* bill that did not match the look and feel of the original was immediately suspect. My fear is that way too many people today can be swayed by counterfeit miracles, signs and wonders because the church is not familiar with and demonstrating the real thing as we should! There have always been counterfeits, and they will clearly continue. But that does not negate the power and authority Jesus' church has been given by our King himself to carry out his mission. Counterfeits will never bring glory to God. The real thing *always* does.

As the church expands, it will carry with it both the words of Jesus including the good news of the kingdom (Jesus' rule and reign, his lordship, his kingship) and the works of Jesus, demonstrating the inbreaking of his kingdom by correctly and fruitfully exercising his authority. (Again, I talk about our God-given authority in Chapter 1). The Book of Acts shows us that, as the church grows, it does so by rendering the kingdom of darkness more and more impotent. It is critical to remember that the church is a fellowship of people who are first and foremost surrendered to God – they (we) are citizens of heaven (Philippians 3:20) – the kingdom of light (Colossians 1:12-13) – subjects of the King of all kings and the Lord of all lords (Revelation 19:16). The heavenly kingdom advances and is ruled by heavenly authority.

In over 35 years of ministry, I have witnessed incredible things as the kingdom of Jesus broke into people's lives and set them free. I've watched God lengthen a leg to match its partner. I've seen him heal a foot. I've witnessed him heal a grapefruit-sized tumor in a 90-year-old woman's abdomen (confirmed a day later by the hospital). I've seen him miraculously heal a woman of daily migraines. My own father was healed of a stroke. One of my colleagues watched God literally raise his uncle from the dead in Nigeria (and the man went on to live for several years, preaching the gospel and using his own coffin as a object lesson!) I've seen people delivered from anxiety, depression, drugs, gambling addiction and multiple people freed from alcoholism as Jesus completely took over their lives. I could go on – but I simply want you to understand that God is still in the business of tearing down strongholds (2 Corinthians 10:3-5), delivering people and wowing our world with miraculous healings as his rule and reign advances, person by person, soul by soul, family by family, people group by people group.

Fellowship Demonstrates Kingdom Relationships

"And all the believers met together in one place and shared everything they had" (Acts 2:44, New Living Translation).

In the kind of fellowship we're describing, family members take care of each other. The love they have for each other speaks volumes to everyone around them. Remember, Jesus teaches us all,

"So now I am giving you a new commandment: Love each other. Just as I have loved you, you should love each other. Your love for one another will prove to the world that you are my disciples" *(John 13:34-45, New Living Translation).*

Everyone who witnesses the quality of love each member of the fellowship has for one another, ultimately sees Jesus. And while low hanging fruit people will certainly be awed as they sense God's presence, and will find the inbreaking of Jesus' kingdom rule and reign more than convincing, I have found that this element of love in fellowship speaks most powerfully to nearly everyone.

We do not love and care for one another out of some kind of agenda – that is not devotion but commitment. No, this love and care is driven by the heart. We care for one another because we authentically love one another as family.

Fellowship Demonstrates Kingdom Priorities

"They sold their property and possessions and shared the money with those in need" (Acts 2:45, New Living Translation).

Because we love one another as a family, we practice kingdom priorities with each other. The early Christians sold their "stuff" so they could take care of one another's needs. Self-care is a kingdom priority. Selfishness is not. The kingdom leads us to an appropriate, Spirit-led, love-based self-sacrifice to meet each others' needs. This is precisely the kingdom culture Paul describes to the Corinthian Christians when he writes,

> *"Of course, I don't mean your giving should make life easy for others and hard for yourselves. I only mean that there should be some equality. Right now you have plenty and can help those who are in need. Later, they will have plenty and can share with you when you need it. In this way, things will be equal. As the Scriptures say,*
>
> > *Those who gathered a lot had nothing left over,*
> >
> > *and those who gathered only a little had enough'"*

(2 Corinthians 8:13-15, New Living Translation).

Fellowship Drives People to Worship and Makes Strangers "Family"

"They worshiped together at the Temple each day, met in homes for the Lord's Supper, and shared their meals with great joy and generosity" (Acts 2:46, New Living Translation).

Though the growing numbers of believers were followers of Jesus the Messiah, they still felt beautifully bound to the Father's house! The Temple was their place of daily public prayers, and they desired to stay consistent in that practice. The Temple was their place of public teaching, and they loved hearing, reading and learning the Word of God. The Temple was their place of public worship, especially since their historic faith and their pursuit of their Messiah was now fulfilled in Jesus. How could they *not* worship? This fellowship was a unanimous and harmonious community in their desire to pray, learn and worship, and it was still very much a part of their daily life together.

This fellowship also continues to meet in each other's homes on a regular basis. They participated in The Lord's Table together – remembering their Savior's sacrifice that both paid the penalty for their sin with his broken body (the bread), and opened the way for an eternal New Covenant relationship with God with his own shed blood (the wine). They ate meals together – truly enjoying an ever-deepening familial bond with each other. And they experienced great joy and generosity. The fruit of this fellowship was growing. Think about how such an experience can impact low hanging fruit people!

Fellowship is filled with God's Praise and Impacts the World

"...all the while praising God and enjoying the goodwill of all the people" (Acts 2:47a, New Living Translation).

As I write this chapter, I am actually overcome with the wonder and joy of it all! Can you imagine this life we are describing? Think of all we have said so far. And this is to be the norm *on this side of heaven!*

The fellowship of believers are a people who are driven by love. Genuine and all-encompassing love for God and for each other (Matthew 22:37-40). The presence of God is very noticeable in their midst. There are regular demonstrations of Jesus' kingdom authority. The members of the fellowship have everything in common, taking care of each other's needs. They center their daily life around prayer, teaching and worship in the Temple. How could they not be filled with God's praise?

But here is the key: the mission of this fellowship is to take the good news of Jesus kingdom to the world – beginning in Jerusalem, and in all Judea and Samaria, and to the ends of the earth (Acts 1:8). And the world around them is watching! The people around them see the kind of love we are describing. They see the kind of care they have for each other. They are witnessing how different is this community of faith in Jesus. They are seeing the power and authority of Christ as his kingdom breaks into the kingdom of this age. They see the public prayers, teaching and worship of this fellowship. And as all of this is put on display to those around them, the world is wooed to their Savior!

Compare what we are describing to most local churches you know. Do they look like this? They *should!* This is the prototype! But alas, my description a few pages back is more accurate today. This has to change, or we will be severely limited in reaching all the low hanging fruit people the Holy Spirit has already prepared around us.

Fellowship is the Vehicle for Evangelism and Disciple Making

"And each day the Lord added to their fellowship those who were being saved" (Acts 2:47, New Living Translation).

May I be perfectly honest? Referring to the idea of people surrendering to Christ every single day, I've heard many pastors over the years say something like, "Acts 2:47 was a first century phenomenon..." I think that's a colossal cop out. I have not seen this in my own ministry, but I do aspire to such a goal! God has not altered his purposes or his plan. The scripture is abundantly clear that our God does not change:

> *"I am the LORD, and I do not change. That is why you descendants of Jacob are not already destroyed"* (Malachi 3:6, New Living Translation).
>
> *"Jesus Christ is the same yesterday, today, and forever"* (Hebrews 13:8, New Living Translation).

> *"So don't be misled, my dear brothers and sisters. Whatever is good and perfect is a gift coming down to us from God our Father, who created all the lights in the heavens. He never changes or casts a shifting shadow"* (James 1:16-17, New Living Translation).

> *"The grass withers and the flowers fade, but the word of our God stands forever"* (Isaiah 40:8, New Living Translation).

> *"Long ago you laid the foundation of the earth and made the heavens with your hands.*
>
> *They will perish, but you remain forever; they will wear out like old clothing.*
>
> *You will change them like a garment and discard them.*

But you are always the same; you will live forever" (Psalm 102:25-27, New Living Translation).

"Lord, through all the generations you have been our home!

Before the mountains were born, before you gave birth to the earth and the world, from beginning to end, you are God" (Psalm 90:1-2, New Living Translation).

God does not and has not changed. Jesus does not and has not changed. The Holy Spirit does not and has not changed. God's Word does not and has not changed. We know Jesus' deputization of us in the Great Commission has not changed. I believe Acts 2:47 teaches us what we should actually expect as we live out this kind of fellowship. And if the Holy Spirit is indeed preparing low hanging fruit people all around us all the time, I believe most of us would be surprised at how soon a church on mission as described above could realize that expectation. Are you ready? More importantly, are you willing?

Putting It Into Practice

Let me close out this chapter by asking you to prayerfully consider some questions. Take your time and mull these over. Take them back to Jesus and answer them to him not to me:

1. What would it look like to live this way in your own personal walk with Jesus?
2. What would it look like for your family to live together both privately and publicly like this?
3. What would it look like for your church LifeGroup or other small gatherings to function like this?
4. What would it look like for your Sunday gatherings and other ministry events to be a demonstration of this?
5. What would happen in your own city, town or village if your church actually functioned like Acts 2:42-47?

6. What would happen in your region if the churches in your city, town or village were of one mind, heart and fellowship in this lifestyle?

7. What steps will you now take to make this fellowship a reality?

CHAPTER 11
Final Thoughts

Then I saw a new heaven and a new earth, for the old heaven and the old earth had disappeared. And the sea was also gone. And I saw the holy city, the new Jerusalem, coming down from God out of heaven like a bride beautifully dressed for her husband.

I heard a loud shout from the throne, saying, "Look, God's home is now among his people! He will live with them, and they will be his people. God himself will be with them. He will wipe every tear from their eyes, and there will be no more death or sorrow or crying or pain. All these things are gone forever."

And the one sitting on the throne said, "Look, I am making everything new!" And then he said to me, "Write this down, for what I tell you is trustworthy and true." And he also said, "It is finished! I am the Alpha and the Omega—the Beginning and the End. To all who are thirsty I will give freely from the springs of the water of life. All who are victorious will inherit all these blessings, and I will be their God, and they will be my children.

"But cowards, unbelievers, the corrupt, murderers, the immoral, those who practice witchcraft, idol worshipers, and all liars—their fate is in the fiery lake of burning sulfur. This is the second death."
(Revelation 21:1-8, New Living Translation)

LOW HANGING FRUIT

Every time I read about the great multitude around the throne from every tribe, language, people and nation, my eyes fill with tears. The scene has done that to me for years. I have a similar response when I read Revelation 21. The church of Jesus Christ is not just spinning its wheels. We are indeed all moving toward the great consummation of Jesus' kingdom. It's real. And it's coming.

My concern is about today's church – especially in the West. Oh, there are congregations that are striving to live out the things we described in this book and they are enjoying its fruit. But far more of them are not. The reality that the church in the West is in trouble is very sobering; however, I want you to see that it's the *institutional* church that is waning. The faithful church of Jesus that is made up of people who are passionate and active in finding, reaching and discipling the kind of low hanging fruit people introduced in this book is not in trouble at all. My own experience bears this out.

I pastor a small band of modern day disciples in Central Florida. My church family is relatively new, planted only a few years before I am writing this book. But I see in that group some incredible things. I see some who are new to the Christian Faith and are learning the principles we've outlined for the first time. For them, this kind of active Christianity is normal. I see others who have spent their lives in other churches where life was more about traditions and programs. They are genuinely born again, but they are now having to both unlearn some ministry patterns, and then learn or relearn these principles. And, I'm very excited to say that there are still others on the journey with us who are low hanging fruit people!

It still surprises me that such a small church – a congregation that doesn't even own its own building – can have such a huge kingdom impact. We recently reviewed all that God has done so far, and the incredible list of kingdom opportunities he is now laying before us and we're in awe. This congregation of less than 50 on a Sunday is outpacing congregations many times our size and resources in making disciples and leading people to spiritual maturity and fruit. This stuff works!

Prepare yourself, understanding the mission and the authority Jesus has already given you to accomplish it. Regularly study the scripture and become intimately familiar with the many examples God has given us in the New Testament on reaching people for Christ. Then put the principles

Final Thoughts

I outlined into practice and start building intentional, redemptive relationships as you identify low hanging fruit family members, friends, coworkers and neighbors. The Holy Spirit might introduce you to someone you've never met on this journey, but most of your low hanging fruit relationships are already there. Be bold and pray with people. Make the most of every opportunity to turn the conversation in a spiritual direction and watch how the Holy Spirit regularly set you up for the "spike." Live a life of genuine, Jesus-style love and lavish it on those around you. Learn how to share your faith, because the Spirit will indeed give you opportunities to do so. And then take time with your low hanging fruit friends to memorize scripture and watch how the Word of God transforms all of you from the inside out. Finally, begin helping your church family to live out the real fellowship described in Acts 2:42-47. Don't make it academic – demonstrate it for them. Make your own household like those of the first Christians. Some people will join you quickly. Others will be later adopters. And still others will resist (or even oppose) you because you threaten their definition of "church." Expect it all – but do not relent. You are not alone. You have a paraclete – a helper (John 16:5-11). The Holy Spirit was given to us for this very purpose. And I guarantee he knows how to handle every obstacle people or the devil may attempt to toss in your way.

I don't know if you are already eagerly on board with what I've taught here, or if you are one of those who must first deconstruct some of your "churchianity" so that you can build a fruitful kingdom mindset. But the destination is the same. Don't be discouraged by where you or your church are right now. Be encouraged that Jesus' original plans still work and are designed for people just like you. Just begin. Step out in faith and ask the Holy Spirit to show you the low hanging fruit people he has already prepared in your life. They are there, you may just have been looking past them all this time.

Gracious Heavenly Father, I thank you for the readers of this humble text. I am grateful for the brief opportunity you have given to me to influence their witness for your kingdom. Now please take what I have invested and bring it to fruition. I pray that they will be anointed by your Spirit for the task. I pray that they will be quick to understand and contextualize the principles of this book to their own lives and witness. I pray that they will readily identify the precious low hanging fruit people the Spirit has already made ready in their lives. And I pray that you will guide and enable them to see real, kingdom success as they connect with these souls for your purposes. I pray that what they have learned will become part of their everyday lifestyle.

I also pray for all the low hanging fruit people my readers will encounter, both at first, and in the future as they continue to grow and prosper in these ideas. I pray that your Spirit will connect these precious souls with people who will genuinely love them and invest in their lives for Jesus' sake. I pray that these precious souls will find Christians and a church that look like the one in Acts 2. And I pray that the results we all see together are like those seen by that church – that you are adding *daily* to the number of real, modern disciples of Jesus because of our collective efforts.

Now, Holy Spirit, help my readers to step out in faith and actually begin doing what they have learned. Nag them, relentlessly but lovingly, so that they cannot simply put this book on the shelf with others whose truth remains unapplied. Take them by the hand and lead them, step by step, into the glorious and exciting world of disciple making. And give each one a steady stream of souls in their lives you have already made ready to receive both the gospel and the spiritual formation that comes with a Jesus-oriented relationship. Grow your kingdom, King Jesus. And use each one of us as your instruments to get the job done.

I pray all this to your glory. Amen and amen.

May God bless you richly on this journey!

OTHER BOOKS BY JOHN KIMBALL

Disciple*Making*: Helping Local Churches Understand What Disciples Are and How to Make Them by John Kimball and Gayle Buford (Minneapolis MN: NextStep Resources, 2019).

Church Revitalization in Rural America: Restoring Churches in America's Heartland by Tom Cheyney, John Kimball, Jim Grant, Rob Hartgen & Chris Irving (Orlando FL: Renovate Publishing, 2018).

Transitioning Your Church: How to Bridge a Pastoral Change by Stephen Gammon, Ron Hamilton, Tay Kersey, John Kimball, Carlton Walker and Ed Whitman (Lake Elmo MN: FORESEE Publications, 2011).

Church Constitution Handbook: Writing, Reviewing & Revising Your Church Constitution and By-laws by Stephen Gammon, John Kimball and Karen Sloat (Lake Elmo MN: FORESEE Publications, 2009).

Countdown to the Mission Field: Launching Short-term Missions Teams from Your Church by John Kimball (Columbus GA: Brentwood Christian Press, 2002).

www.ingramcontent.com/pod-product-compliance
Lightning Source LLC
Chambersburg PA
CBHW050909160426
43194CB00011B/2345